PRAISE FOR
ROUND ZERO

"As much coverage as the NFL Draft receives, it's remarkable how many misconceptions there still are. Andy fields stories from some of the greatest figures in NFL history to show how unique the pre-Draft process is. *Round Zero* will give you the inside stories from the true angles of the NFL Draft."

— TRENT DILFER,
former 1st Round pick & Super Bowl champion quarterback

"As a long-time Division-1 Athletic Director of over fifteen years, I see firsthand how intense, complex, and unique the NFL Draft process can be every year. Andy has assembled some of the NFL's great Draft stories directly from agents, players, coaches, and general managers. Fans get an inside look at every angle and situation the Draft has to offer. *Round Zero* pulls the curtain back and leaves no stone unturned."

— DAVE HEEKE,
*Vice President & Director of Athletics,
University of Arizona*

"The annual National Football League Draft has ballooned into an event unto itself, a rite of spring bridging one season to the next and capturing fan attention in a way no one could have imagined just a decade ago. To understand the Draft from the inside requires the insiders' knowledge and perspective Andy Phillips reveals in *Round Zero*."

— RICH DESROSIERS,
Chief Communications & Content Officer,
Pro Football Hall of Fame

"The NFL Draft is the biggest event of the league's off-season calendar and there is no spectacle like it. Yet what goes into it and how it all happens remains among sport's greatest mysteries. Andy goes deep to demystify the experience and tell some of the best stories I've read about the Draft. He talks to so many key participants and observers, the power brokers who make it go. Finally, *Round Zero* offers a real-life glimpse into the Draft to provide the full picture."

— IAN RAPOPORT,
NFL Network Insider

ROUND ZERO

ROUND ZERO

ZERO

INSIDE THE NFL DRAFT

Andy Phillips

Hatherleigh Press is committed to preserving and protecting the natural resources of the earth. Environmentally responsible and sustainable practices are embraced within the company's mission statement.

Visit us at www.hatherleighpress.com and register online for free offers, discounts, special events, and more.

ROUND ZERO

Library of Congress Cataloging-in-Publication Data is available.

ISBN: 978-1-57826-972-3

Printed in the United States

10 9 8 7 6 5 4 3 2

All statistics and accolades quoted in *Round Zero* are drawn from Sports-Reference & Pro-Football-Reference.
Check them out yourself at www.pro-football-reference.com and www.sports-reference.com/cfb/.

CONTENTS

INTRODUCTION
Firsthand Experience

C OLLEGE GRADUATIONS BRING excitement to those involved. Families and friends will gather to celebrate their loved ones as they enter a new and exciting world. If someone who has never been to a graduation asked you to describe one, what would you say? You would likely say it's a celebration of a milestone in front of a crowd full of people in business attire listening to names being read off a paper and cheering as said person walks across the stage into their new life. What if that same person asked you to describe the NFL Draft? Is it possible the majority of your explanation would mirror a college graduation? The answer is "yes." Why is it that millions and millions of people, not even related to those walking across the stage, will watch the NFL Draft each and every year, yet approximately zero people will head to a random graduation where they don't know a soul? The answer can be summed up in two words: "passion" and "hope."

Passion for an NFL team is something most graduates don't generate for other people. Those who know them may become fans of their work ethic, personality, or drive, but you won't buy a ticket to *Student A's* chemistry lab on Thursday. The NFL, of course, thrives off its fans. Fans are the reason the NFL is worth billions, and its stars are worth millions. Fans adore and idolize teams and players from afar with the utmost passion. Without the fans buying jerseys, tickets, and television networks that carry the games, the NFL would just be the most competitive intramural league in the world.

Next is hope. Hope is as strong of a word as there is in the English language because it can often be a savior for those who need it. You may lose your job, get a flat tire in the middle of nowhere, or get dumped by your high school sweetheart. Yet for four hours on Sunday, you can turn on your team's game and forget about your problems. It will all be okay, at least for a while. The feeling of hope that fans feel for the NFL is something that is rarely, if ever, replicated. The NFL Draft specifically evokes hope to its core because it's a moment where almost every fan base believes they just drafted the next great player for their franchise, and it begins all of the *"this is our year"* talks.

Trust me: I grew up in Michigan as a Detroit Lions fan. The Draft is historically the most positive time of the year for

Lions' fans. That is why millions of people will travel to the Draft and why millions more will watch it on television. It's not much different than a graduation. There is still someone reading names off a card in front of a nicely dressed crowd. There are still people walking across the stage in celebration as their lives change before their eyes. However, the NFL Draft offers passion and hope for those not even directly involved.

Everyone has his or her own view on the NFL Draft. Whether it's a fan's point of view, one heard from a sports radio host, or an opinion read in the local newspaper, we all have our own thoughts on the NFL Draft each and every year. The goal of this book is to take you away from the opinions of *94WIP* in Philadelphia, the *New York Post* back page, and Uncle Frank's expertise on why the Jets *"need to fire everyone!"* We are going to peel back the curtain on the beloved NFL Draft but let me first share my angle of the NFL Draft from my own unique experience.

After completing my four years of eligibility at Central Michigan University (CMU) where I started forty-three-consecutive games on the offensive line earning All-MAC honors twice, I headed off to EXOS in Los Angeles to train for the 2015 NFL Draft. I had no clue I would meet a person there who would turn out to be incredibly important to me a few months later. That guy was Brett Hundley, star Quarterback from UCLA, who was also training at EXOS.

After California, I returned to CMU to compete in the Pro Day where I performed better than a lot of people expected. I ran a 4.99 forty-yard dash, bench-pressed 225 pounds twenty-six times, and broad jumped 9'2", among other drills. I remember leaving my Pro Day and calling my agent, Carter Chow. When Carter heard my numbers, he told me, "You may have just gotten yourself drafted." Carter is an incredible person who never sugarcoated anything to me. When he said that, I knew I had a legitimate chance at my ultimate dream. We both knew with my small size (6'2") and short arms (south of 31 inches), it would take a great Pro Day to draw some attention. We both felt I did just that.

Once Pro Day was over, I had just over a month to transition from "combine shape" back into "football shape." As the Draft was approaching, I started receiving a few calls from NFL scouts, mostly just to get my contact information for the Draft weekend. However, there were a few teams that showed the most interest towards me. Those two teams were the Chicago Bears and the Atlanta Falcons. A Falcons staff member ran the offensive line drills at my Pro Day and showed an incredible amount of interest, talking about how their new scheme would be heavy zone run and insinuated that my skill set would fit in perfectly. Before the first round of the 2015 NFL Draft, I even received a phone call from the the Bears' offensive line coach, Dave Magazu. Although we all knew my name would not have a shot at being called until day-three, it was surreal to get any sort of attention just hours before the first round began. I remember Coach Magazu wishing me luck and stating that it was going to be an incredible weekend for me. Talk about giving me some confidence heading into the weekend! Confidence to the point we were debating on having Bears and Falcons hats in-house ready to go if selected.

Finally, on day-three of the NFL Draft, I sat in my parents' home in Lansing, MI surrounded by family and friends while Carter communicated with me from California. Tensions and nerves got higher as we started to approach the last few rounds. The Bears did not have a seventh-round pick, so after they used their final pick in round six, we knew I would need to sign their post-Draft if Chicago was the team for me. The Falcons were now my hope as they not only had two seventh-round picks, but Carter also told to make sure my phone was ready for them. The final round of the NFL Draft would come...and go. Now we waited...and waited...and waited. Ten minutes went by...then twenty...then thirty. It was stressful and awkward to say the least. My phone went radio silent. The only communication I had was with my former college offensive line coach, Butch Barry, who was then the Tampa Bay Buccaneers assistant offensive line coach. He told me he thought he could get me a tryout in Tampa Bay, but it would come with no guarantees. When the only possibility you think you have is a pity-tryout from your former coach, you lose confidence in your NFL future lightning fast.

Over an hour later, Carter and I finally had a good talk. Not great, but good. After failing to get offered even an undrafted free agent contract, I accepted a rookie camp tryout invite with the Green Bay Packers. All of their drafted rookies, their signed rookie free agents, and twenty-five tryout invitees would all attend a rookie camp the following weekend. Carter said we had a few tryout options, seven total, but he felt Green Bay was best option because they hadn't drafted an offensive lineman. The good news was that not every NFL team holds their rookie camp on the first weekend. Carter was also able to accept my invite to the Kansas City Chiefs' rookie camp for the weekend after in case I did not make it in Green Bay. As a tryout guy, I wasn't guaranteed to last beyond one practice much less sign a contact.

I remembered that the Packers selected Brett Hundley in the fifth round, so I texted him to let him know I would be seeing him soon. When I arrived in Green Bay, I could already tell I had passed the first test. I was dressed correctly. It may sound simple, but it matters for a tryout guy who will only be evaluated if noticed the right way. I wore a button-down collared shirt, brand new jeans, and dress shoes. When I got off the plane in Green Bay, Matt Klein picked us up. Little did any of us know that he was head coach Mike McCarthy's right-hand-man at the time, but looking back, I'm happy I dressed appropriately.

When we arrived at Lambeau Field, they took us to our lockers. We walked past the man, the myth, the legend himself—Aaron Rodgers. I felt he was the best player in the league for a while and he was just coming off an MVP season. Not knowing how stars reacted to rookies, I had no clue if he would even look at us, but he did. What he did next always stuck with me. He looked over at us, smiled, and said "Slappies" in a very cool and funny manner. We all chuckled nervously. It was the first of the many times Aaron would show he cared about everyone on the team, not just the other stars.

What happened next, was not expected either, but this time, I was not as amused. All of the rookies began finding their lockers...HUNDLEY 7 (drafted)...RYAN 47 (drafted)...HENRY 85 (undrafted/signed). I was thinking, "Where is PHILLIPS?" And then I realized we tryout guys were not in there. No, we were on our own in the Away Team's locker room. That hurt, but there was no time to feel bad for myself. Instead, I turned my feelings into motivation When I saw my locker name tag—PHILLIPS 57—it was still an incredible moment, even though it was not in the locker room had I imagined. However, I hadn't come for that moment. I came to compete.

We went through physicals, meetings, meetings, and more meetings before finally arriving at the hotel around 9:30 p.m. on Thursday night. The bus would be arriving again at 6:00 a.m. Friday to head over to the stadium for the first practice. That left us with two choices: rest up to be ready to roll in the morning for the biggest job interview of our lives or study the playbook they just gave us. For me, there was only one option, and I wasn't the only one who felt that way. Brett Hundley and I studied that playbook for hours. We figured that as a quarterback and center, we would need to know the offense the most and be on the same page with protections, run schemes, and snap counts.

The next day came and went. I had plenty of reps, played well, worked hard, and proved one thing better than the others—I studied. I studied a lot. And do you know what Brett and I did when we finally got home on Friday night? We studied again. I knew that install like the back of my hand and it paid off for me the following day.

The next day at practice the center reps were not split evenly between the two of us centers. No, I earned the majority of the reps the next day because I did these three things: I took command in the huddle and at the line of scrimmage; I communicated the calls to everyone around me loud and confident; and I finished every single play down the field. That's right, the undersized center from mid-major CMU earned the majority of reps over the power-five University of Oregon center.

And then it was over. I didn't know what to expect. I knew I had done well, but I didn't know how well. They had not drafted any offensive linemen that year, but they signed three immediately after the Draft. I was not sure if they needed me, but I knew I did not want to get on that flight to Kansas City the following week. I saw an article where Brett was interviewed, and he mentioned those study sessions. There is no way of knowing if by him showing faith in me also gave the coaches faith in me, but I appreciated Brett if it did. I signed a contract with the Green Bay Packers the next day and was the only tryout player to do so.

I also want to thank Brett for the pair of Adidas shoes he gave me because, remember those dress shoes I mentioned earlier? Yeah, those were the only shoes I brought with me. Those Adidas shoes always had special meaning to me. The next day, I had a new locker and a new number. Going forward, when I walked into the immaculate Home Team locker room I saw it—PHILLIPS 77.

Over the next five months, I created memories that I will never forget. A few guys and moments are the ones that still stick out to me to this day. First were the fellow offensive linemen. Corey Linsley was a great mentor and friend to me, and I appreciated all of the rides he gave me and our conversations. David Bakhtiari and Bryan Bulaga were always there for any question I had or advice for how a rookie should act. Josh Sitton and T.J. Lang were there to emulate to the fullest. I practiced behind two of the best guards in football at the time. Why would I not study their every move? They treated me like a little brother: tough, honest, and supportive. And then there were the defensive linemen, Mike Daniels and B.J. Raji, who would help me beyond measure. Mike led by example, going harder than anyone on the field even in walkthrough. He was also the biggest pain in the rear to block. B.J. helped me out more than he knows. I told B.J. one day that I liked doing one-on-one pass rush drills against him because it helped me so much to go against the best. Most veteran players wouldn't take an extra rep with an undrafted rookie at the end of the period during training camp, but once I said that, B.J. always seemed to take the time to go against me. And there was also Julius Peppers. I had his jersey as a kid! The first time I had to block him was in a 3rd Down Team Period during Training Camp. I blocked him well—very well. I think I surprised everyone on the field, including Julius and even myself. Later in practice when we went to one-on-one pash rush drills, I will give you one guess who lined up across from me? You know it—Julius Peppers. He got me that time. No question about it. For me, that showed how competitive he was, and it was no surprise he was still playing at such a high level for his age at the time. Julius has since retired and finished his career with 159.5 sacks, which currently ranks fifth on the all-time list. Finally, I want to thank Aaron Rodgers who made it a point to talk to the undrafted, rookie center. Whether it was quizzing me on plays during walkthrough, yelling "great job!" after a big block, or even sitting at the breakfast table one day to get to know some of us better, he had a huge impact on me. My last practice as a Packer was before the final preseason game and I had the privilege of playing center for him for an entire drive (which we scored on). It was a moment I will never forget. I often wonder if he knew that was going to be my last practice and he wanted to give me that moment. Thanks to this book, I was able to ask him.

I was cut after the final preseason game, and I would never play another down of football. I was lucky enough to be a part of one of the best organizations in sports for four months, play four NFL games in incredible stadiums (Lambeau Field, Heinz Field, and Gillette Stadium), ride bikes down the infamous

"Dream Drive" during Training Camp, and make memories I would never forget.

Now, when I watch the NFL Draft, I have a completely different view because of my experience. There is an old saying that "you don't know what you don't know" and that surely applied to me. I had no idea before this experience that a team could seem as interested in a player as the Bears and Falcons seemed to be in me, and then after the Draft, want absolutely nothing to do with them. It was eye-opening to say the least. Now every year before the first round, I remember getting that call from Coach Magazu and I wonder how many other players will get a similar call that day. I also look back after day three of the Draft and wonder how many guys are just sitting, staring at their phones waiting for news, any news, about if they will have a future in football.

I was an underrated, undrafted, tryout offensive lineman from Central Michigan University in my NFL Draft experience. Can you imagine the experiences and stories other players who were drafted high or not, decorated agents, legendary coaches, and wheeling-and-dealing general managers would have? Wonder no more. It's time to uncover the stories, angles, and nuances of the NFL Draft from the people directly involved with making it one of the greatest events on the sports calendar each year. The old saying goes that history tends to repeat itself, and that is no different for the NFL Draft. When you read the Draft stories in each section, you will gain insight into the real scenarios that take place in not only those specific Drafts, but those in the future as well. Because of the stories here, you now will have an understanding about why certain moves are made, or not made. It's by no means an answer key for future Drafts, but it is certainly a cheat sheet of knowledge. Without further ado, let's begin.

SECTION I

THE
AGENTS

NFL AGENTS ARE incredibly valuable during the NFL Draft process, yet most people have no idea what exactly they do. The idea that they simply negotiate contracts couldn't be further from the truth. While it is certainly a part of their job, a lot takes place before agents have the opportunity to negotiate contracts for their clients. I was represented by an incredible agent who you will read about in this section, and I can tell you firsthand how important he was during my process.

In this section, you will learn how an agent identifies potential clients to represent. Unbeknownst to most, agents won't simply take as many players as they can get each year. Getting the right number of players to represent is crucial to any agency. Sure, more players that make an NFL roster will result in more money for the agency, but not every player represented is a slam dunk to make a final roster. Each player an agency takes on is an investment to the agency that only pays off if the client makes an NFL roster. To ensure each of their clients maximize their potential during this time, most agents take on a limited number of clients each Draft class. They then focus all their efforts on getting them ready for the biggest job interviews of their lives, which includes NFL training camp and making it through final roster cutdowns.

Once identified, it's up to the agent to help the client make the best decision about where they should train pre-Draft for the NFL Scouting Combine and Pro Days. This is a process that each agent handles different. The player typically will have a say in this, but the agent helps by making recommendations. When it comes to Draft Day conversations with teams, it's easy to imagine that agents are on their phones screaming and pounding the table for their clients with teams. That is not how it goes. There is a time and place for having these conversations, but not in that manner. Learn how agents communicate with teams to help not only sell each client's value, but also to gather information to help paint a picture to their clients about the most likely outcomes on Draft Day.

Agents often have a background in law, and unfortunately, can be viewed in a negative light by the public. In reality, they truly believe that communication and relationships are the most important qualities in their business. I could feel how much the agents cared for their clients and how hard they worked to impact their futures in a positive way. I believe this is the section that will be the most eye-opening for readers. It is the angle of the Draft that is the least discussed, therefore, the least known. Read how four of the best NFL agents operate and understand what is happening behind closed doors when you watch the NFL Draft in the future.

CARTER CHOW
All About Relationships

C ARTER CHOW IS a partner at Yee & Dubin Sports and the CEO of Red Envelope Sports. He has been a certified contract advisor with the NFLPA since 2007. Chow's father, Norm Chow, was a decorated offensive coordinator in the college ranks and spent three years in that role in the NFL with the Tennessee Titans. Coach Norm Chow was also the head coach for the University of Hawaii from 2012–2015.

The younger Chow grew up in the game of football and learned firsthand the importance of building and maintaining relationships in the sport. Many of the relationships he has nurtured throughout his career as an agent were formed early on in his life in a very organic fashion. In addition to early relationships, Chow spent a year working for an NFL team when he got out of law school. It was during that time when he met many scouts, coaches, and members of the media who are still working in the NFL to this day. It's an experience that Chow describes as invaluable because he was able to experience the way teams talk and act which is something that Chow took with him to the agent side, even though he had no intention of working in the agent business at that time.

Chow and the team at Yee & Dubin Sports always look for a certain type of prospect to represent. They aren't a firm who simply takes on anyone or everyone. They have a process to find the right players for them. Chow says it's a process that has been refined over time by which they look for three specific traits:

> "The first is whether the player has the ability to play on Sundays. That's obviously important, right? There are a lot of good college players, but I think the art of what we do and what personnel people do across the league, is being able to project what a player will be at the next level. There are a lot of awfully good college players that never have pro careers, and that could be for a variety of reasons. Maybe it was the system that they played in in college or the level of competition that they played in in college. There are a lot of different factors and variables that have to be

considered. They could be the greatest person in the world, but if your client does not have the ability to play on Sunday, it is hard to maintain a sports agency. We need to find players that, whether they're drafted or undrafted, have the ability to make an NFL team."

How exactly does Chow find out that answer? It goes back to relationships. In addition to watching a ton of tape to identify players himself, Chow has been fortunate throughout his career to build great relationships with scouts and coaches who often refer him a player based on the type of player and person they know Chow wants. Chow says that has been, without a doubt, the best way to get clients over the years. It still doesn't make a kid a slam dunk to play on Sundays, but they typically have the correct personality traits Chow seeks. From there, Chow and his team do their own work on a player to continue to make their best decisions going forward.

Chow shared that he has found that a player must have one trait or skill he does exceptionally well to make the NFL. Not good, not average, but exceptional. One can be lacking in other areas, but he better have one quality that makes him special. There is so much competition for these roster spots and the competing players will almost always have a special quality to set them apart. A competing player must have something that makes him invaluable to the team come roster cutdown time.

Chows elaborated on the second trait he looks for in players:

> "Second, I'm looking for good character individuals to work with. I think every successful agent will tell you that, but when I say "character" I'm looking more for intangibles like coach ability, humility, what kind of locker room guy is the player, what kind of teammate, is he going to put the work in—those kinds of things. We certainly don't want to have to worry about guys that are going to create messes in the middle of the night or in the offseason. That's kind of a given, but character for me means those things. However, the only way to try and identify that in a potential client is to really get to know the player and his family, talk to people in the building that have worked with him, and talk to scouts that have gone through the school and have met with the player and his coaches. For NFL teams, it works the other way as well. Teams understand that if they draft or sign a Carter Chow client, the odds are high that the player is a hard worker who will keep his nose clean."

The third trait that Chow looks for is simply whether the player is a good personality fit for him and his firm. They work with a limited number of players each year and are so intertwined in their lives that their personalities must fit together during this process. Chow has found a lot of success over the years at finding those three qualities in quarterbacks, offensive linemen, and linebackers. Make no mistake though, he and his team represent players at all positions from schools across the country. When it comes to the actual Draft, Chow said the real work has been done prior to the first team being on the clock. They have identified a handful of teams that could potentially draft their clients as well as teams that would be a good landing spot if a player is not selected during the Draft. What's fascinating is the way Chow watches the Draft. He doesn't watch it necessarily the way a client or a fan would. He admits that, of course, when his client gets drafted it is nice to call them and celebrate the achievement. However, what he is really doing during the Draft is watching how teams' depth charts and positional needs change so that if he has a client that goes undrafted, his team can wisely identify a team or teams that will give the client the best opportunity to compete for a roster spot. Chow even believes that when you look at the backend of the Draft, it shows that it may actually be better for some players to go undrafted. That way, agents have all the data to help the player make more informed decisions about possible teams for tryouts.

With that, I can speak firsthand about my experience being an undrafted player who was represented by Carter Chow. Chow identified a few teams before the Draft that could be good fits and teams that would possibly draft me based on pre-Draft conversations. However, once the Draft was over, those identified teams went radio-silent and apparently wanted nothing to do with me even as a free agent. Thankfully, Carter, as he explained above, was identifying potential landing spots before and during the Draft. As the handful of tryout opportunities came in, Chow called me and explained why the Green Bay Packers were the best tryout camp to attend for me. They hadn't drafted any offensive linemen in the 2015 NFL Draft and there has been a history of players from the Mid-American Conference succeeding there. The Packers also prided themselves on being one of the best developers of offensive linemen in the NFL. To Chow's credit, he was exactly right. It's very hard as a tryout player to go somewhere and get noticed enough that the team will want to sign you. Fortunately, Green Bay saw something with me after rookie. I credit Chow's ability to read the Draft to place me in the best possible situation to find success. It also wouldn't surprise me if the reputation of past Chow clients didn't give Green

Bay even more confidence in signing me because they knew I possessed the qualities of a Yee & Dubin client.

One Yee & Dubin client who Chow worked with directly epitomized everything that Chow looks for in a client: Julian Edelman. Edelman is now retired and remembered as a three-time Super Bowl champion, a Super Bowl MVP, and one of the most prolific postseason wide receivers the NFL has ever seen. Back in the spring of 2009, not many people saw that coming, but Chow and the New England Patriots both knew there were special traits to work with. Chow recalled:

> "I don't think anyone really knew what position Julian would play in the NFL. He played quarterback at Kent State and we had a relationship with the head coach there. The coach had actually referred us to another player on the team at the time, so we're watching tape and this little dude just kept running around making play after play after play, and my partners and I were like, 'Hey, let's talk to the quarterback.'"

Chow and his partners weren't the only ones who were curious about Edelman's potential. The Patriots sent multiple coaches to work him out, attempting to see just what skills Edelman would possess outside of the quarterback position.

Chow recalled some scouts laughing at the time believing
Chow and his agency were wasting their time with Edelman
because there was no chance he was going to play quarterback
in the NFL. Chow still remembers the call where his partner,
Don Yee, told a general manager that Edelman could even
play defensive back for them in a pinch because he was that
athletic and smart. To Edelman's credit, he was willing to do
anything asked during the pre-Draft process and worked as
hard as possible to put himself in a position to succeed.

The Patriots took a chance on Edelman in the seventh
round of the 2009 NFL Draft with the 232nd overall selection,
knowing Edelman would draw a lot of competition if they let
him get to free agency after the Draft. Ironically, according
to Chow, Yee & Dubin already had an established client with
the Patriots whom Edelman would make sure he became very
close with.

> "My firm represented Tom Brady and he and Julian
> established a relationship. The stories that you heard
> about Julian coming out to California and just kind of
> waiting at Tom's doorstep for him to ask him to throw
> with him early in his career are true. Julian would do
> anything that he needed to do to get an opportunity
> and, in my opinion, had a Hall of Fame career."

Chow said he looks for players that don't just have that competitive fire and work ethic during the pre-Draft process and through training camp, but all the way through their careers. It is the second and third contracts where everyone makes the real money. I can attest that Edelman kept that fire well into his career. When I was training for the Draft at EXOS in Los Angeles, we always used to play ping-pong before, in between, and after workouts. Edelman was coming off his first Super Bowl win against the Seattle Seahawks in Super Bowl XLIX and he showed up to begin offseason training about a month after. He walked in that first morning as a Super Bowl champion still representing his roots in Kent State gear. I will never forget playing him in ping-pong because he was as intense playing ping-pong as he was playing football. I was leading in a game to fifteen by a score of 11-7. Edelman rattled off the final eight points of the match to bury me 11-15. He was intense. He would dive for a ball, and would often come out victorious in that room. Between that fire and his passion during workouts, the career he had is no surprise. And it's even less of a surprise that Chow is constantly searching in his future clients for those exact same traits that Edelman possessed.

Chow didn't grow up dreaming of being an agent, but he grew up in football and was exposed to the business of football at an early age. It's not a coincidence that he understands the importance of relationships after watching his father work in the business for so many years. Whether with coaches, scouts, or players, Chow attacks those relationships with his own intensity, work ethic, and passion. While Chow has the three traits he searches for, it is those three traits also within Chow that will have his clients singing his praises long after they are done playing, as I am to this day.

CASE DONAHUE
Working a Region

C ASE DONAHUE IS considered young in the agency
world, but he and the team at IFA are far from inex-
perienced. IFA has a great strategic plan, which works
well because of their ability to customize it to be sure it fits the
prospect perfectly. The plan is also in place to ensure that IFA
is at their best for the prospect, which in turn benefits IFA in
the long run. Donahue shared:

> "At IFA, we're more of a boutique firm, which allows
> us to be agile and nimble where we need to be. With
> our client list, we have about thirty to forty guys that
> are active, and our recruitment process affords us to
> be really selective. We're not waiting outside locker
> rooms at the SEC and we're not going about it the old
> school way with runners. We have three agents on

staff and all of us work collectively to find prospects, recruit them, and then put a strategy in place to hope to go sign them. In a perfect world scenario, we'd prefer to sign about five guys per year just because we try to have a five to one to staff ratio, and so we really try to focus on that personalized attention and allow these athletes to maximize their opportunities on and off the field."

Donahue emphasized that they understand the jump from college to the NFL can be overwhelming and a difficult adjustment for players. It's a big reason why they choose to have the ratio they do at IFA.

The IFA's goal is to help maximize their prospect's potential and if that means giving each of them extra attention and consideration, they are happy to do so. Donahue and IFA also strive to recruit a certain type of player.

We try to target guys that check off a lot of our boxes. First of all, we look for local talent because if you learn more about the industry there are a great deal of agencies on the West Coast, many are on the East Coast, you'll find most firms are based out of LA, Atlanta, Florida or New York. So, with that in mind, we built IFA in the Midwest with the goal of putting a fence around this part of the country. There's a lot of great talent that comes from the area that generally gets overlooked. We try to locate talent in the local schools such as Minnesota, Michigan, Iowa, Iowa State, North Dakota— those schools because those players usually possess a blue-collar mentality that is similar to ours as an organization. They may not be all glitz and glamour, but their priorities are in order. They're here to play football, build a legacy, and create generational wealth.

IFA's goal is to identify prospects whose values align with their company. This practice allows them to be able to work together seamlessly because the common goals are the same. There is an old saying that NFL stands for "Not For Long." Understanding that, IFA focuses their time and resources on players who bust their tails to get to their second contract.

Once they sign their clients, it's time to make sure they receive the proper training. Another unique element about IFA is that they don't have just one or two facilities to send their guys to train for the NFL Scouting Combine or their Pro Days. They are willing to send their clients all over the country knowing that each client has different needs and IFA's singular objective is for them to be able to maximize their performance. According to Donahue...

"If I tell you 'Go train here' and you hate your trainer or you don't want to be in the city or it's too hot or

it's too cold, then you're going to be p***** off and
you're going to have a bad Combine or have a bad
Pro Day. What we do from a Combine training process is we collect feedback from all thirty-two NFL
teams and organize it into one document saying, 'this
player needs to work on his strength, or he needs to
work on his speed, or he needs to work on his agility'
and figure out the pros and cons about our players
through direct NFL feedback and then based on that
intel, we provide our recruits or our rookies with our
best recommendations on where we think they need
to go train."

Being able to use real feedback from the very organizations
that their prospects will be interviewing with is a massive
recruiting tool, but also a great business model. It allows IFA
clients to address areas of concern prior to getting into an NFL
camp, rather than finding out once they are already under the
microscope.

   On top of physical training, IFA also has former Minnesota Vikings' general manager, Jeff Diamond, on their staff
to assist players with preparing for pre-Draft interviews with
teams. They have bi-weekly calls set where they help prospects
with everything from their posture to eye contact while on the

whiteboard. Jeff's expertise is a huge asset because a prospect can make or break themselves in an interview room with a team's brass.

To give a specific example of how a Draft Day scenario can go, Donahue explained how a recent client of theirs, Rashod Bateman, ended up with the Baltimore Ravens. Heading into the 2021 NFL Draft, the former Minnesota Gophers' wide receiver was projected to be selected in the late-first or early-second round. From Donahue's communication, they felt that there were two teams most likely to select him. One team picked well before Baltimore and they figured the other would need to trade up for him, which at one point they heard was a good possibility. The first team ultimately decided they preferred a different style wide receiver as they continued to build around their young quarterback. That left the second team, but due to some unknowns that took place prior to the start of the Draft, Donahue believes the team's plan to move up for a wide receiver was altered. With those two teams out of the hunt, Baltimore gladly took Bateman with the twenty-seventh overall pick in the first round, which was a pleasant surprise for both Donahue and Bateman. "He's loved it ever since, but the Ravens never thought they would get him. Bateman was very excited to be drafted [by Baltimore], but it was probably our last thought that he would have gone there given all the information that happened within the Draft that night." The communication process with NFL teams can help give agents and their prospects a general idea of the teams that are showing the most interest in their clients, but much like anything else that is dependent on other factors, the plan can change in a second. Donahue and IFA have a very flexible process that allows them to maximize their client's potential, but in terms of finding the correct prospects, they are more specific to their core values. That combination helps IFA find incredible success in the Draft and will allow them decades of future success in their attempt to put that fence around the Midwest region.

LEIGH STEINBERG
Master Communicator

L EIGH STEINBERG HAS over four decades of experience representing NFL players. The NFL Draft is the start of many of Steinberg's relationships, including representation of eight first overall picks during his illustrious career. Steinberg explained that before he can be there for his players on Draft Day, he must figure out which players to represent because agents won't, and frankly can't, take on just anyone.

"The process involves profiling a potential client so that I understand their value system, their heart, their character, their background, so I know it's all fit into a practice that emphasizes the concept of role models. Is this someone who would be willing or excited about retracing their roots and going back to the high school, collegiate, and professional community and setting up programs such as a high school scholarship fund? Which Tua Tagovailoa just did at his high school in Hawaii. A college scholarship fund, the way of reuniting with the alums from the school and finding mentors in that group to help for second career. A charitable foundation at the pro level in their professional city, that encompasses meeting business figures, political figures, and community leaders and put him on an advisory board and then executed program tackling some need that they know in the community. Warrick Dunn put the 175th single mother and their family into the first home they'll ever own by making the down payment. We call the program 'Homes for the Holidays.' So, the question is, is this person a self-starter?"

Steinberg's goal is to take a high draft pick and help them not just build a Hall of Fame football career but to ultimately allow them to be set up for a Hall of Fame second career when their playing days are over. Steinberg and his team teach players to understand the power of branding while they have their platform. When talking with the parents, guardians, or role models of potential clients, Steinberg wants to know much more than just about their football careers. He's looking for people who have been on mission trips or were actively involved in their high schools. All those qualities will help show Steinberg the type of character a prospect has. Aside from obviously being a hard worker, Steinberg also wants to be sure his clients have a specific quality, which is being able to look adversity in the eye and remain calm, cool, and collected.

Steinberg referenced an example of a quarterback battling through adversity after throwing a few interceptions and being able to "adopt a quiet mind, tune out all extraneous stimulus, and elevate their level of play to take a team to and through victory." Steinberg has made a point to emphasize the quarterback position throughout his career because quarterbacks typically have what it takes to be a Steinberg-repped player.

"I've probably represented 150 quarterbacks over forty-eight years. That was my first client, Steve Bartkowski, and over the years it's been first rounders like Tony Eason and Ken O'Brien and Neil Lomax and on and on and on. That's basically what I look for, and by doing a thorough screen upfront, then I know if I've got the type of client ready for a fairly sophisticated practice that requires them to be ambitious in a second career. The quarterback position, that player, is going to always sign the largest contract of any position in football, they're going to be terrific from a standpoint of role modeling, they have an active endorsement market, and ultimately, at the end of the day, have more branding potential and that's going to lead them into (successful businesses outside of football)."

Another factor that plays into who to represent is how many to represent. At the end of the day, each player will require a certain amount of work, branding, coaching, and training. It isn't necessarily a more-the-merrier business because even agents only have twenty-four hours in a day. Potential first-round picks, especially, garner so much attention that taking on too many could lead to an agent being overstretched. In Steinberg's opinion, he knows the maximum number for him. From Steinberg's experience representing four first-rounders several years, that's the most he would ever do.

The key to success for an agent and his clients really boils down to communication on all levels: agent to player, agent to team, team to player, etc. Being able to have great dialogue ultimately will help a client not have a big surprise on Draft Day by who or where they are picked, but also it allows an agent to know what teams his clients could have the best career with. For a client to end up having the best possible career to maximize their abilities, Steinberg emphasizes how much that is reliant on the player ending up in a good situation. The situation must have stability at the ownership spot and a game plan for the future success of the organization. They need a general manager with a history of drafting well and constructing an NFL roster capable of competing year in and year out. Lastly, you need the coach that can put it all together and execute the organization's plan. Steinberg believes New England Patriots head coach Bill Belichick is the best he has ever seen at putting together a game plan that puts the players on his roster in the best positions to succeed. When you combine those components, a player will have the best chance to find success.

Steinberg's key to success is to communicate with his clients about which teams are highly interested in them. At the end of the day, the goal is to have a few teams show great interest, rather than have even all thirty-two teams be just moderately interested. It's up to Steinberg and his team to find those teams, educate his clients, and help them know exactly what to expect going forward. If one of those teams happens to meet all the criteria of a great franchise that Steinberg stated above, then that is a cherry on top.

"The communication goes many different directions. First of all, we're preparing an athlete for all the testing and training that they're going to have to do. In the modern agency, the agent is responsible for the training of the player, sending him to a training facility. We're also responsible for the ultimate game plan. There are no rules in scouting. No completely obligatory events. Someone can go to the Combine or not. They can work out at a Pro Scouting Day or not. They can take trips at the end of the process to franchises or not. It's all a matter of volition on each client's behalf. So, you lay out a scouting game plan and then where there's intense interest, there's a fair amount of communication between me and our staff and teams."

Steinberg not only helps change his clients' lives, but he's been instrumental in the Draft's contract negotiation process over the years.

Steinburg understood early on that the NFL isn't competing against each other in the grand scheme monetarily, but rather competing against all other forms of entertainment that could take its fans away from consuming the NFL such as other sports, television shows, and even Walt Disney World.

"I said, 'We're doing this the wrong way.' Instead of having acrimonious, hostile, individual player negotiations that make everyone look greedy and push fans away. Let's keep that private instead of having acrimonious negotiations for collective bargaining that pit millionaires against billionaires and alienate the public, because it's like Marie Antoinette. Let them eat cake. Really our focus ought to be working collaboratively to explode the television contracts, to build stadiums that have multiple ancillary revenue streams, to figure out merchandise and memorabilia that's high, high quality, to propagate fantasy sports, betting, and every other ancillary revenue flows. If you have that, then it enabled me to go to the Jerry Jones' and Bob Krafts' of the world and to say 'Let's be partners' in a figurative sense in this process. One of my sources of information is owners themselves, because they tend to be significantly less cautious and much freer to talk about how they feel about players."

That communication and trust between an agent and owner can come from a variety of different experiences. For Steinberg, one of his relationships with a current NFL owner came about in an unorthodox way.

Forty-five years ago, Steinberg had season tickets to the
Raiders games and he happened to sit next to a young gentleman at the time named Mark Davis. Mark was the son
of Al Davis the legendary owner of the Raiders at the time.
Little did Steinberg know that Mark Davis not only would
have his father's ear, but he would also end up becoming the
owner of the Raiders himself one day. Having that resource
has paid dividends over time for Steinberg as I am sure
it has for Davis as well from a communication and trust
standpoint.

What's nice for Steinberg is that he doesn't have to be or act
like a scout who knows every little thing about every player's
game. He will have an idea of the player's abilities, sure, but he
is largely dependent on the feedback he receives from teams.
There is a massive amount of communication between teams
and agents during this process.

Teams have the right to draft whatever available player they
want when it's their pick. Steinberg understands that, but he
also understands that teams need to know if a player is favor-
able to going to their team. The communication goes both
ways. The team will want to know about a player's medical
history and character to form their opinion, just like a player
would want to have a good feeling about a team's coaches,
system, or even location. In the end, the teams still hold the

power on whether they draft a player and trusting an agency is also part of it.

With Steinberg's wealth of experience representing more than sixty first-round picks and hundreds overall, teams have a good idea at the type of player Steinberg represents by now. With that, he knows how this time of year works and wants to be certain he is giving his clients the best advice during the process. If teams raise any concerns about one of his clients, it's up to Steinberg to try and resolve those. An example of that would be if Steinberg's client ran a bad forty-yard dash time that did not reflect the speed teams saw on game film, his advice to the client would be to continue to train for the forty-yard dash and supplement that by running the forty-yard dash at his upcoming Pro Day. The feedback is very active during this time, but not always predictable. Steinberg explained with a few examples.

"There was a year when Cleveland was deciding between Tim Couch and Akili Smith, my client, and so we were talking with Cleveland all the night before about which one they'd picked, and we didn't really know until that next morning who they would pick. Conversely, a team like the Chiefs will say 'We really have an interest in Patrick Mahomes and we may

have to trade up to get him. What are you hearing?'
Teams will be really honest with me as long as I don't
cross fertilize the results. Kansas City doesn't want
the Chargers or the Saints or the Texans to know if
their interested and it's my job to be a neutral broker
at that point or an advocate of a certain team, but not
to cross fertilize information, so they'll be very honest
about what they're thinking."

By having great dialogue and building that trust, Steinberg can
gather information that helps his clients prepare for teams that
they could expect to be drafted by. At times, you must tell a
player that a team is just not interested, but in one of Steinberg's
cases, the team was more interested in his client's former college
teammate. The client Steinberg was representing was Alabama
wide receiver Jerry Jeudy who was very excited about the potential to land with the Raiders at the time. Having that relationship
for decades with Raiders owner Mark Davis mentioned above,
Steinberg was able to gather information that the Raiders
actually preferred Jeudy's Alabama teammate Henry Ruggs III.
Having this information allowed Steinberg to prepare his client
and focus on the hot teams that were more likely to pick him.

The Raiders did spend the twelfth pick in the 2020 NFL
Draft on Alabama wide receiver Henry Ruggs III, while Jeudy

would go fifteenth to the Denver Broncos. Having the ability to prepare a player before the Draft is a strength of Steinberg's. It's not always the most fun or easiest part of his job, yet he understands the importance of the communication process because even if it's not the news the player wants to hear, being honest and informative can bring clarity and calmness to a stressful day.

Steinberg shared a story from 1995 about a quarterback named Rob Johnson. As he went through the Draft process, two hot teams were identified for him—the Jacksonville Jaguars and the Buffalo Bills. Jacksonville was the hottest team having indicated the possibility of taking him in the first round. That was until the week of the Draft when they acquired quarterback Mark Brunell. Steinberg and Johnson knew they wouldn't have done that if they were still planning on using a first-round pick on a quarterback. Buffalo on the other hand would use their first-round pick on an offensive guard named Ruben Brown out of the University of Pittsburgh so they believed Johnson still had a shot of ending up there. It's during this time that Steinberg educates the client and his family about the space he could see his client going. The Buffalo Bills would absolutely draft a quarterback, but his name was Todd Collins, not Rob Johnson. But it was those hot teams that still were key as Jacksonville would still wind up drafting

Johnson with the first pick of the fourth round. Having those teams with intense interest will always help you have a better idea where a player could land, even if it isn't in the round they hoped it would be.

As discussed earlier, players also have opinions about whether they want to go to a particular team or not but having an opinion and taking action are two different scenarios. One of the most famous Draft stories was University of Mississippi quarterback Eli Manning's refusal to play for the then San Diego Chargers. It is very known that the Chargers would take Manning still, the New York Giants would select North Carolina State's Philip Rivers, and the teams would eventually swap the two not long after. What people don't think about is the third quarterback taken in the first round that day, Miami (OH) University's Ben Roethlisberger who was represented by Steinberg.

"The year Ben Roethlisberger is drafted there's trade talks going on because the New York Giants covet Eli Manning, and I've talked enough with Ernie Accorsi at the Giants to know that they think he's a generational player. They think he's one that only comes along so often, and whatever happens they're going to try to get Manning. Well, I also know from talking to San

Diego that they were the coaches in the Senior Bowl, and they had Philip Rivers (there) and they fell in love with Philip Rivers and there was a bonding there and they were destined to get him. So, I know those two things going in, but trade talks are faltering all the way to the day of the Draft. So, Tom Coughlin calls (Miami (OH) Head Coach) Terry Hoeppner. Tom Coughlin is the head coach in New York and says, 'If we come down to the fourth pick and you see that Manning goes first for the Chargers and Robert Gallery goes to the Raiders and Larry Fitzgerald goes to Arizona, then when our pick comes, we're taking Ben.' So, Terry tells that to Ben, so that sets up the expectation that that's where he's going because the trade hasn't come together."

Steinberg explained the frustration it would cause because Draft time is not real time. Every second feels like a minute while teams are on the clock deciding how to use their pick. Time gets elongated and patience is not the most common quality for clients and their families. The frustration is caused by the assumption that teams should know exactly what they want so if they haven't made their pick fast, they must be working on a trade. That is not always the case.

Steinberg explained how informing is all part of the preparation with a client.

"I'm telling Ben this trade is going to happen in my view, and it may not happen before the Draft, but it will happen on Draft Day. That sequence of players goes where we just said and now you come to New York and the trades not done and Ernie Accorsi (is) saying publicly it's not done and Eli Manning is up (on stage) looking completely dissatisfied because San Diego feels compelled by the draft value of Manning, who's the top draft value, and by their fan pressure to take Manning, but they don't really want Manning, and I know that,' Steinberg chuckled. 'I know they wanted Rivers and vice versa. So, we now are sitting there backstage in Madison Square Garden waiting for the pick at a table with Ben, Terry Hoeppner, his parents and waiting... and with like fourteen minutes and fifty seconds done in their turn, up steps the Commissioner to the podium and announces there's been a trade and a swap between San Diego and New York and New York with the fourth selection has selected Rivers and they then swap picks. POP! The arrow goes out of the balloon and you're sitting there and boom. Now I know that there's not another team that's likely to take him until Pittsburgh or potentially Buffalo."

Steinberg and Roethlisberger would sit for seven picks waiting for Pittsburgh to finally select Roethlisberger with the eleventh pick of the first round. Remember, this is Draft time where seven picks can feel like an eternity. Steinberg knows that the letdown of the New York rug being pulled out from under Roethlisberger at the last minute really put a dagger on the mood when he was selected by Pittsburgh, but as Steinberg would say, "It was a marriage made in heaven."

The quarterback position is so reliant on where you end up and the pieces that you will have around you as a young player that a player refusing to play somewhere can be a concern gor the player's representation. While Steinberg didn't have that happen to him, we go back to the aforementioned Akili Smith to a close scare for Steinberg.

At a luncheon prior to the Draft, the buzz started to circle that the Cleveland Browns would be selecting Kentucky quarterback, Tim Couch, with the number one overall pick. Now Steinberg knows Smith will all but certainly be selected by the Cincinnati Bengals who Steinberg did not have the best experience with in the past. Being that communication is key for Steinberg, before Smith was selected, he wanted to inform the family of the Bengals' history with quarterbacks and how due to the Bengals depth chart Smith would not be the starter right away. Next thing Steinberg knows, the entire Smith family started a prayer circle ultimately deciding they will accept going to Cincinnati. Steinberg couldn't help but to laugh recalling that story because he isn't sure what he would have done if the result of the prayer circle was different! An underrated part of going from being a good agent to a great agent is your ability to assess risk. Not risk in the sense of true danger, but risk for the betterment of your client's wellbeing. That means allowing players, even if they are invited to the Draft, the opportunity to not go and instead stay around their loved ones and away from the cameras. The last thing Steinberg wants is one of his clients having all the cameras on them as they are the last player in the Green Room at the Draft. Steinberg explained how he has been helping players find places for gatherings, even back in the 1990s, turning a hotel into what looked like his office so his clients could have plenty of room for family and friends. Recently, they have gotten those sessions sponsored. For example, Patrick Mahomes' Draft Day party was was paid for by Panini according to Steinberg.

When quarterback David Klingler was selected by the Cincinnati Bengals in 1992, Steinberg also learned the hard way that your Draft emotions don't always mix well with cameras. Shocked that the Bengals would take Klinger, Steinberg's true reaction was caught on camera as he said in his words, "Oh no. Oh my God, Mike Brown. Not Mike Brown, again," Steinberg said referring to the Bengals owner.

To this point Steinberg has represented eight number one overall picks and has seen twelve of his clients elected to the Pro Football Hall of Fame, one being quarterback Warren Moon whom Steinberg gave the presenting speech for at the Hall. To see the player be validated by the greatest honor an NFL player could receive to stamp their legacy in history meant the world to Steinberg.

The truly great agents, such as Steinberg, wear many hats leading up and through the NFL Draft, but it all starts with the process. The process of finding the right person, not just the right player. The process of making sure that every player you bring on aligns with your values, with your reputation. Your job as an agent is to represent and sell your client, but for the great ones, their clients will be representing and selling the agent in return by how they carry themselves.

VINCENT TAYLOR
Impacting Others with Powerful Belief

V INCENT TAYLOR HAS been a certified NFL agent since 2005. He started Elite Loyalty Sports in 2007, where he is currently the CEO and an agent. Taylor and his team at Elite Loyalty Sports have had many success stories and none more notable than helping Trent Williams sign the largest contract for an offensive lineman in NFL history with the San Francisco 49ers in 2021.

When it comes to finding future NFL players to represent before the NFL Draft, Taylor says that his guidelines have changed over the years as he gained wisdom in the business. Not to mention, when you are newer in any industry you don't often have the luxury to be picky. The right to get picky often comes as you prove yourself over time. Now that Taylor has proven himself in the business for as long as he has, he has certain traits that he looks for in his clients that he knows will make them successful. "I want to work with people that have good character, people that have a good work ethic, and people that understand the space. What you are is not a promise, it's a privilege. Guys that get that are really humble and blessed to be in this position."

In terms of where he will go for talent, Taylor says he will go anywhere in the country, but he also says it must make sense from a financial standpoint if it is outside his typical area. He doesn't understand where the myth came from that NFL agents have no limits on spending money because he said the business is not friendly in that regards. Taylor typically works the southern part of the United States, going from anything that borders Texas, over to Florida, and even up into the Carolinas. To get Taylor to go outside of that area would have to make sense, but it is on the table.

When it comes to positions, Taylor has made great work with offensive linemen, as noted above with Trent Williams. However, there was one specific client that helped Taylor step into that niche by the experience they went through together. "I've been blessed to work with and see how to transition an offensive lineman from good to great or make a blank tape a hit album. And it came from Jason Peters and watching his transition being a tight end to one of the best offensive tackles (in the NFL). Being really involved in his development in the offseason and watching the tape study, I would say offensive line is something that I hit the lottery with Jason. So, with that came a lot of education and it's spilling over into the defensive line play."

Taylor represented Georgia's do-it-all defensive lineman Travon Walker in the 2022 NFL Draft. Walker was deemed one the biggest risers in recent memory during the pre-Draft period. A riser to the media and public means that he went from being viewed as a mid-to-late first round pick at the start of the pre-Draft process by many mock Drafts and pundits, to then being talked about as the potential number one overall selection by the end of the pre-Draft process. Mind you, that doesn't necessarily mean that he was a riser in the eyes of the actual teams because, for all we know, they may have rated Walker that high from the beginning. Regardless, understanding the trenches—the offensive and defensive line positions—helped Taylor during the ascension of Walker. Walker aced the pre-Draft process from dominating the NFL Scouting Combine to getting invited to and traveling all over for team visits prior to the Draft. Walker would end up being selected by the Jacksonville Jaguars first overall in the 2022 NFL Draft.

Taylor credited his ability to spot talent and athletic intangibles as one of his best traits as an agent. He was a former high school football player in the state of Texas and then played basketball at the collegiate level, so he understands and can process these traits as well as anyone. When he first started in the business, he didn't have the capital or relationships to fall back on. Instead, he had to trust his eye and find the diamonds in the rough. A great example of this came in 2006 when Taylor signed a wide receiver from division-II University of Central Missouri named Delanie Walker. Taylor was able to find Walker and build a great relationship with him. Part of that relationship was built on trust. That trust was called upon very early on in Walker's NFL career after he was drafted by the San Francisco 49ers in the sixth round with the 175th overall pick.

"He's one of my first clients and he gets drafted, does everything right. We get picked, and the first day of (minicamp) he calls me and says they put him at tight end the very first day. (They) didn't warn me, didn't warn him, we had no time to prepare for it. He called me already, 'Vince, get me the bleepity-bleep out of here!' I said, 'What's wrong?' He says, 'Man, they put me at tight end and even changed my number, man!

They got me blocking these 270-pound dudes, somebody busted my lip today, man! Get me out of here!' "

Mind you, in that same Draft the 49ers had selected Vernon
Davis, a tight end out of Maryland, with the sixth-overall
pick in the first round. It wasn't the ideal spot to be moved to
for that reason alone. Taylor knew he had to talk Walker off
the ledge because the last thing he wanted was for his client
to want out of the current situation when it had just begun.
Taylor said, "I just listened to him and then my natural instinct
kicked in. I was like, 'Delanie, you can do it, man. Listen,
alright, let me talk about you,' and I just start (talking) about
his traits and why you're tough enough. All you got to do is
figure out how to stop these guys. They weigh more than you,
just for a second. I said, 'Man, you can do it. You're from one
of the roughest hoods known to man.' He's from Pomona."

About three days later, Walker would call Taylor and not
only said he was good, but he knew he found a great new
home at tight end. Walker certainly would find a home as he
would go on to become a three-time Pro Bowl tight end and
be considered one of the very best of his generation at the
position.

When it comes to training, Taylor has three or four facilities where he likes to send his clients because they have gained

his trust over the years. He also understands that each client might be better off in certain locations geographically based on family and atmosphere. If a guy would get easily distracted by night life entertainment, Taylor knows the prospect would be better off not training at a facility in Miami, FL. It's all about building a trusting relationship and educating the clients to help make the best decision for their process.

Taylor truly believes in building relationships with each of his clients and ultimately wants the very best for them. He shared one of the very best quotes in the entire book because I could tell it was authentic and genuine. "If football doesn't work, I at least want to be somebody that never gave up on you, and then we will do something together that'll change another life."

It's a powerful and sincere statement. Taylor wants to continue to build Elite Loyalty Sports into one of the greatest agencies in the world. In doing so, he keeps the mindset of helping young men change their lives forever. While changing financially and professionally through football is, of course, the main objective, Taylor knows the intangibles in people have the possibilities to go far beyond the field. He strives to be there every step of the way for his clients, even after he is done representing them.

SECTION II

THE GENERAL MANAGERS

A N NFL GENERAL manager, scouting department, and front office are the parties most involved with how Draft Day turns out during the NFL Draft. Ultimately, they are the ones, specifically the general manager, pulling the trigger and making the selections. How exactly they arrive at those decisions is the question.

I only needed to speak with two former general managers to get a fully transparent view of a team's pre-Draft process. After all, if you get to learn from two Pro Football Hall of Famers, why would you need anyone else?

This section of the book is what I was personally the most curious about because it's a precise and detailed process for the one with all the power, which is unbelievably intriguing. How do you even begin to form "the Board?" "The Board" will be referenced early and often in this section since it is viewed as the Draft Day bible for high-end general managers around the league.

To get a grasp on a general manager's process, I chose general topics for questions rather than specific questions to let the masterminds talk for as long as possible.

In these chapters, you will see there is more than one way to pluck a buzzard as both men had some different ways of attacking the process. There isn't one right way to go about it, but I can say one thing for certain: there were certainly a few similarities you will notice that should be uniform across every scouting department and Draft room. If they aren't, it may explain why some organizations struggle on Draft weekend. The Draft is hard; don't make it any harder on yourself than it needs to be.

Some people may see this section and decide they don't need to read it because they already saw Sonny Weaver, Jr. execute the greatest Draft in Cleveland Browns history in 2014. However, the rest of you acknowledge that was just Kevin Costner starring in the movie *Draft Day* and realize that maybe, just maybe, everything you see in the movies isn't always an accurate depiction of real life. I suggest you take a peek at this chapter and see how two of the greatest ever took their swings at the NFL Draft with more than three decades worth of combined general manager experience. Don't get me wrong, the movie is fantastic, but I can promise you real life is even better.

BILL POLIAN
Builder of Champions

O CCASIONALLY, A GENERAL manager can strike lightning in a bottle by hitting the target on most draft picks, being in a preferred free agent destination, and having the correct coach to maximize their roster. Rarely, that system will help a general manager have similar success at another franchise. But, to do it for three teams at a high level? That should be impossible, right?

Bill Polian was the architect responsible for taking three different NFL franchises to championship games and two franchises to Super Bowls, one which eventually hoisted the Lombardi Trophy. What makes this feat even more impressive is that Polian was never in a *"Honey, we're moving to _____!"* type of destination. Polian wasn't the general manager in sunny Los Angeles or Miami. He wasn't the general manager in massive-market New York or Chicago.

He wasn't even the general manager of a traditionally great franchise in an unpopular location such as Green Bay. Polian was the brains behind the best years Buffalo, Carolina, and Indianapolis respectively have ever seen post-merger. Polian was the man in charge for three of the Bills' four consecutive Super Bowl runs. He was the head man for the expansion Carolina Panthers, who by year-two were playing in the NFC Championship Game. He was also responsible for bringing Peyton Manning to Indianapolis, where he would rewrite the record books and bring home a world championship.

While you think you have an idea about what it takes to build a champion after watching Kevin Costner in the movie *Draft Day*, Polian can confirm that you should take what you see there with a grain of salt. "The only thing that was realistic about the movie *Draft Day* was the fact that on Draft weekend, you eat a lot of bad food. That was the only thing that was accurate."

With that being said, where does a general manager even begin to build? The true foundation is the system. The system will determine how your handle business pre-Draft, which is really the most important time for personnel staff.

"On Draft Day, we had a saying which we abided by totally, which was to say, 'Let the Board speak to you.' When our turn came, we're basically going to take a player that was there in that round that we had targeted. If such a player wasn't there our first option was to trade out, and if that option didn't come about then we're going to take the next best player on the Board regardless of position. That had already been decided through the pre-Draft process. So, on Draft Day the only question that was involved, which involved the head coach, was do we trade up or do we trade down? And he had a very important voice in that decision. There were basically five people involved in that decision: the college director, the overall personnel director, the assistant GM, the head coach, and myself. The college director in our configuration did all of the pre-Draft research on what was appropriate to pay and not to pay to move X-spots in Y-round. We each had a chart that showed us that. (It) was based on five-year historical perspective, not the Jimmy Johnson point system; we didn't use that, but this was our version of it, and then those discussions would take place, if not on the clock, well in advance of our pick if we thought that a trade was a possibility, and the coach had a lot to say about that."

Polian will be the first to admit that he and the coaches didn't always agree in these situations, and even disagreed quite frequently. In situations with Pro Football Hall of Fame head coach Tony Dungy in Indianapolis, it usually was a difference in philosophy. Dungy preferred to accumulate more draft picks, where Polian would rather figure out a way to get the players they targeted, even if that meant giving up a few of their picks. Famously, Polian won a few of those arguments by landing Colts' legends Bob Sanders and Robert Mathis, but Polian said he was by no means always correct in those scenarios. Frequent disagreements about a prospect or trading value became the reason Polian and his system focused so heavily on having these conversations during the pre-Draft process. There was one thing that Polian demanded they did not have on Draft Day. "I hated chaos. I wanted quiet. I wanted the television sound turned off. I wanted quiet conversation. No table banging. None of that. None of the stuff that's depicted by the media."

To be sure chaos would never enter the equation on Draft Day, Polian and his staff made sure they had their Board built to reflect exactly how they viewed each prospect. For starters, in Polian's system, they had to determine the round in which they believed a player belonged. To do this, they used their complex and detailed grading system, which was made up of college film, NFL Scouting Combine metrics, medical information, and character evaluations. Typically, they would have fifteen to eighteen players with a grade in each round. In fact, Polian's system found that over a decade span, there would be an average of about eighteen prospects with first-round grades each year. With the understanding that not every team would have the exact same eighteen players with those grades, they would estimate that anywhere from twenty-two to twenty-four players would have legitimate first-round grades across the league. Think about that for a second. Thirty-two players will be selected in the first round, so that means that the backend of the round is likely made up of players that did not have a first-round grade. Some of the players with second-round grades would end up going in the first round, which leaves even less of the targeted players potentially available in round two. That theme will continue to compound each round any time that players go ahead of their grade, which is why trading back is so popular amongst the best front offices in Polian's opinion. Like Polian in Indianapolis, Bill Belichick is a master at this after all those years having such late Draft picks in the first round for New England. Polian explained...

"As he says to himself, 'I'm getting the same player in the front end of the second round, and maybe even the very same player in the front end of the second round, and I pick something else up to do it. Let me give you my guru saying which I often used on ESPN, 'When the need line and the talent line (the grade line) crossed, make the pick. If they don't, pick the best player."

When teams stray away from Polian's saying, that's precisely when a 'reach' happens. Polian discussed how there is a difference in what the media portrays as a reach and what is an actual reach. "(Television guru's) definition of reach is, 'You took player-X six spots higher than we think he should be taken.' That of course, means nothing. It's nonsense. But the true definition of a reach is, 'You take a player whose grade tells you that he doesn't belong in that round, but you have a need, so you take him anyway. Reaches almost never worked out. Almost never."Polian clearly put an emphasis on value—value on a prospect per round, value on moving up for their targeted players, and of course value on trading future picks. In today's era of the NFL, certain teams are deemed "all in" because they trade future assets (draft picks) for current players, or better referred to as known commodities who can help them immediately. General manager Les Sneed and head coach Sean McVay are famous for this since arriving in Los Angeles with the Rams.

Polian explained, "Let me take you through the whole equation starting with square one. The metrics, and I'm giving you our metrics, which my friends in the league, my former colleagues verify to me are still accurate today. The vast majority, over seventy-five percent of the players who make a difference for you, make a difference in winning, meaning, in our power parlance, are blue and red players. Blue players are Peyton Manning, Dwight Freeney, and Marvin Harrison, right?"

Polian's metrics told them that seventy-five percent of blue-chip players will be drafted in the first three rounds. That means you better hit on those picks if you want to win because those are the rounds where you would get the players who would make the biggest difference in winning. Rounds four and five would be used to build the depth of the football team. The final two rounds, six and seven, you would get a quality player every other year if you were good. If you weren't, you will virtually strike out every year in those rounds.

For Polian, giving up one or more first round picks in a trade would only be considered on a very specific and special occasion because, in doing so, you gave up years of club-control of your star players. Drafting a player in the first round meant having their rights for at least five years, not even including the option to Franchise Tag them after their rookie deal ended. In order for Polian to give up that right, he not only preferred to have at least three years of club-control left on the player's contract, but insisted the player be the key to their team's success schematically as well.

> "Let me give you an example. (Jalen) Ramsey, as good as he is, we would not give up a (first-round pick) for him in Indianapolis because that shut-down corner was not critical to our defense. Conversely, (Joey) Bosa we would surely give up a (first-round pick) for. We would give up two (first-round picks) for Aaron Donald. So, that's how you balance. That's how you look at that equation. Now, the Robert Mathis example, it's a perfect example of using a future draft pick to obtain a player who is a difference maker. We got him in the top of the fifth round, but with a big helmet sticker on him (on their Board). We're all in love with him, but he's a smallish outside linebacker at Alabama State. Small school, PQ's don't really match up. It's only for us so we're saying, 'Yeah, leave him in the fifth. but we better be ready to move if we think there's somebody else that's interested in him.'"

During the fourth round, the Colts realized it would be risky to wait until their low fifth-rounder if they were intent on getting Mathis. Polian had to send an additional mid-round pick for the following year in a trade, which head coach Tony Dungy wasn't initially thrilled with doing for a mid-round guy. Polian convinced him by reminding Dungy how excited he would be to have that pick on the team this season, and not have to wait another year to use the pick. Dungy agreed and the rest is history for the future Colts' franchise all-time sack leader.

Each of the three franchises Polian headed up had very specific Draft stories that helped to define their time there. Starting in Buffalo, Polian had to jump through hoops to get his future bell cow running back in the second round of the 1988 Draft. Polian loved everything about Oklahoma State's star Thurman Thomas and rightfully had him graded in the first round. However, during that time in Buffalo, the team doctor had the final say on where they could ultimately place a player on their Board. In Thomas' case, the doctor was heavily involved in the conversations. Thomas essentially was missing a ligament in one of his knees, which of course caused the doctor to initially fail him all together. Polian and head coach Marv Levy did not want to remove Thomas from the Board, so they asked the doctor to watch a tape of Thomas' prior knee operation to see if he would reconsider. Upon review of the tape, the doctor believed while he would have the risk of blowing it out and missing the year,

Thomas could have a quality career with the proper rehabilitation. Due to the risk, putting him in the first round was off the table. Polian didn't care as long as he could put him on the Board. Finally, after convincing the rest of the Bills' brass to let Thomas be on their Board pre-Draft, the Bills were aiming for him with the fortieth pick. Of course, not everything can go as planned. Not long before their pick, a trainer brought up that he heard Thomas missed practice time at Oklahoma State due to the knee. Polian was not pleased that this was brought up now instead of pre-Draft. As we now know, Bill Polian despises chaos on Draft Day. Polian had a little time and got Thomas' college coach on the phone to discuss and found the coach's answer was quite ironic. The missed practice time had nothing to do with the knee, they had simply wanted Thomas to get some rest during the week. Interestingly, Oklahoma State had the luxury that season to rest Thomas and still have a high quality running back with the first-team offense. His name was Barry Sanders.

The Bills carried on and selected their future star running back right where they wanted to and Polian would land, in his eyes, a first-round value in the second round. What a win for the Buffalo Bills and for Thurman Thomas.

Polian's next challenge as a general manger was with the expansion Carolina Panthers. How on earth do you begin to orchestrate a blank slate of a roster for an expansion team?

For Polian, the plan was quite simple to talk about now, but the "system" referenced here was actually started by Polian in Carolina and later used in Indianapolis.

The NFL required the Panthers to select 40-45 players in the expansion Draft. Polian and his staff figured they could select six to ten players that they believed would truly help the team. Once they selected those players, they made sure the rest were all low-salary players, which was genius. In the first year of the NFL salary cap, the new team on the block would have plenty of money to offer the highly sought-after free agents. The rules would change by the time the NFL's next expansion team arrived, but Polian and the Panthers took advantage of it while they could. The Panthers goal was to use the money to fill out their defensive unit. By doing that, they had the skeleton, the foundation of a veteran team even in year-one. For the first few Drafts, they focused on filling their offense with young, talented players with the likes of Penn State quarterback Kerry Collins, the Michigan State wide receiver Muhsin Muhammad, and Michigan running back Tim Biakabutuka.

The plan worked and the Panthers were part of the NFC Championship game in their second year of existence. In Polian's eyes, the next part of the plan was to turn over the defense because it was getting old and getting old fast. They knew that would happen with the way they handled the expansion Draft and free agency early on, so Polian and his staff we ready. Unfortunately, NFL owners often meddle when the team is close to the Super Bowl. In this case, Carolina's owner at the time, Jerry Richardson, thought the Panthers were one player away from going to the Super Bowl because they were so close. In end, the linchpin of the Panthers' defense was the late,Kevin Greene who decided to hold out for a new contract. Ownership got involved and it all went south, ultimately leading to Greene being traded. They were so close and keeping Greene and drafting some fresh, new defensive players would have put them exactly where they wanted to be. Instead, the defensive leader was gone after only two years, and the initial plan was as well. In all, what Polian orchestrated in Carolina was nothing short of remarkable and would give him the experience needed to make his final, and his best, stop.

When Polian arrived in Indianapolis in 1998, he was at the center of one of the most famous quarterback prospect debates of all time: Manning vs. Leaf.

"I was a 'scouting GM.' I was not an in-the-office-seven-days-a-week guy. I went to two to three games a week. So, I was out seeing the players. Certainly, everybody in the first round and probably most in the second or third. So, when it came time for this December meeting, which is when you first craft the Board for the upcoming Draft, I was familiar with all the top players and had opinions, by the way, but not flushed out opinions, not completely formed. I sat down with the scouts, I said, 'How many like Manning?' Half the room raised their hand. 'How many like Leaf?' Half the room raised their hand. I said, 'Okay, why do you like Manning?', and the answers were rational and well thought out. 'Okay, why do you like Leaf?' and the answer was, 'He's a way better athlete than Peyton Manning! Peyton Manning can't win the big game! He doesn't have a big arm!' it was like, 'Whoa, I didn't ask you why you didn't like Peyton Manning. I asked why you liked Ryan Leaf,' I said, okay, well we clearly have a disagreement, and I'm not ready to break the tie yet and we don't have a coach yet, so to be continued. So, I went to the film guy and I said, 'Give me every pass Peyton Manning and Ryan Leaf threw in their college careers, give me a cut up reel,' and he said, 'We don't do that kind of thing.' I said, 'You do now. If you can't, I'll find somebody who can.' I went back over the film. I probably went back over those two films four times, so that's probably 2000 passes maybe. I'll keep it short. We went through the normal scouting process. I asked Bill Walsh to look at the film and give us an opinion. Jim Mora was our coach, Bruce Arians was our quarterback coach, and Tom Moore was offensive coordinator. They were obviously doing the very same thing."

By the time the NFL Scouting Combine rolled around, Manning was the favorite amongst the Colts' brass, but it was by no means close to being a done deal. Of course, something happened at the NFL Scouting Combine that would further tip the scale in Manning's favor—Ryan Leaf blew off his meeting with the Colts. Polian said that was a huge negative on Leaf, but he told his staff not to crush the kid over it because he felt he was getting advice from his agent to do so. Peyton Manning showed up for his meeting with the Colts the following day, and in classic Manning fashion, he was well prepared.

Polian recounted the meeting, "We sit down he said, 'You mind if I ask you a few questions?' and he took out his yellow legal pad and pencil. We were given twenty minutes to do those interviews. The horn blew, ending the twenty minutes, he stood up and said, 'Well, thanks guys, I really appreciate it. It's been fun and I hope you draft me,' and we shook his hand and he left and walked out of the room, and we looked at each other and said, 'Well, that was nice. He interviewed us. We didn't ask any questions."

Neither quarterback would work out at the NFL Scouting Combine, but both would hold private workouts that the Colts would attend, which happened to be consecutive days. First up was Manning in Tennessee, where he performed tremendously and even destroyed the myth that he didn't have a strong arm. As a matter of fact, after watching Leaf the next day, the Colts believed Manning had an even stronger arm than Leaf did.

Not remembering whether it was at the NFL Scouting Combine or at the individual workout, Polian recalled how Manning told the Colts he would be ready to be at the facility the day after the Draft to begin working. The Colts told him that wasn't necessarily allowed, but Manning insisted they find a way because he would be there. Naturally, trying to compare every possible scenario between the two prospects, Coach Mora asked Leaf if he would be ready to get to work the day after the Draft. Leaf told him he would be on a Las Vegas trip with his buddies the first week and wouldn't get in until the middle of the second week. Polian still recalls seeing Coach Mora's blood pressure rise after hearing that answer.

"When we got on the plane to go home, Bill Walsh had already rendered his opinion, which was Peyton. I said to Jim and Tom and Bruce on our way home, 'Listen if we don't pick Peyton Manning, we're going against everything we believe in because we think that intelligence and maturity and leadership and the ability to process quickly and ability to be accurate and the ability to play big in big games and preparation is so much more important than the physical part of it,' and everybody nodded their heads and said, 'Yes, that's exactly right.' If we don't take Peyton Manning, we're going against everything we believe in. So, I would say at that point it was ninety percent done. We still had the background check to do, and Ryan's background check did not come out well. I'll leave it at that. It just didn't, and so that sealed the deal."

The Colts had Manning come out to have his knee checked out the week before the Draft just to be sure it looked good, and that is when the infamous story took place.

"That's when he came into my office and said, 'You know, I really want to be drafted here and I don't want to go to New York (for the Draft) unless I had that commitment,' and I said, 'Well, you know I can't make that commitment to you now. I got to finalize it with

Mr. Irsay and coach and everything.' So, we agreed that he would call on Thursday and I said, 'You got to keep this secret because Mr. Irsay wants to be there with the Commissioner to make the pick,' and he said, 'No, I give you my word I'll keep it. I'll keep it quiet,' and then he turned to me and said, 'You know, if you draft me, I promise we'll win a championship, and if not, well, I'll come back to kick your a** for fifteen years.'"

Polian was a no-brainer for the Pro Football Hall of Fame, being inducted in 2015. He is the first to mention that the system they developed and used wasn't uniform around the league. To be frank, one system wouldn't fit all organizations because there are so many variables involved. However, having success for three separate organizations is eye-popping. If you're a general manager or an owner with a general manager opening, it would be foolish not to reach out to Bill Polian to soak up any bit of knowledge he has to offer. Three for three is about as bulletproof of a resume as there has ever or will ever be across all professional sports.

RON WOLF
The Wolf of Canton

R ON WOLF IS a member of the Pro Football Hall of Fame, after his career as one of the greatest general managers the NFL has ever had. Wolf is famous for building the Green Bay Packers of the 1990s and bringing the Lombardi Trophy back home to Green Bay for the first time since the trophy's namesake, Vince Lombardi, was the head coach in Green Bay.

As you may very well know by now, not every organization handles the NFL Draft or the specific process the same. When it comes to constructing the Board, there are different philosophies and the one Wolf used in Green Bay was one he was introduced to earlier in his NFL career.

"We had a system that we borrowed and tweaked a little bit when I went to Green Bay from the system that Tommy Prothro had devised with the San Diego Chargers a long time ago. I had first come in contact with that through my time with the Raiders and Al Davis, and essentially, we put a Board together of only those players that we felt could make our football team and we did it by round. Obviously seven rounds, so we had seven and then we had a free agent board as well, but the only people on our Board were people that we had studied and done an extensive film review of their ability to play, and then they got up on the Board. They got put up in certain rounds. The most we ever had on that Board, and it might shock you, is one-hundred and twenty-five, and we never ran out of names, ever. That's kind of how we did."

The system clearly worked for Wolf and the Packers, but the culture needed to be changed in Green Bay. Today, Green Bay has a reputation of drafting and developing talent as well as any organization in football, but when Wolf arrived that was not the case. Long were the days of championships with Vince Lombardi. Green Bay's worst period as a franchise were the years between Lombardi and Wolf, and that was a very long period. It's easier to break organizational habits of a few years than it is to break the bad habits that have been around for decades. The Packers needed a shift in the way they attacked every area of their front office and personnel departments. Wolf did just that, but in a very honest way, even he admits there is something he would have changed.

"If I could change one thing that I did back then, we had too many categories for first-round players, and we spent too much time in that area when the bulk of your team comes after that as you know. That would be the one thing I changed. But, as you're aware, Green Bay didn't have an owner, so we had the executive committee and they would come in and they look for names of very popular players, and they wouldn't be on the Board because we didn't think they could play for us. So, you can imagine that. But as I said, it worked, and we ended up changing the entire culture up there in Green Bay, WI from a loser to a winner. We had an .841-win percentage at Lambeau Field during my time there as a result of this, twenty-five straight wins in Lambeau Field. Things that people, when we got there, never thought they'd ever see again. So, we were very fortunate."

When it came to how much say coaches had during this process, Wolf would work it out with his head coach, Mike Holmgren.

"We gave our coaches like ten guys to evaluate or five guys to go see if you will, and that was all part of the equations. But Mike and I would work that out. Interesting experiences, I got there, and Mike got there. I hired Mike, and we didn't know each other. I didn't know what kind of player he wanted for his system. That first year we kind of stuttered a little bit with it, but once we got past the first year it worked perfectly. We're perfect in our relationship because we realize we're doing one thing: we're picking, in our opinion, the best player for the Green Bay Packers. It didn't have to be Ron Wolf's player or Mike Holmgren's player or this coach's player or this scout's player. It was for the betterment of the Green Bay Packers, and I stressed that, and I also stressed this: you make one exception and pretty soon you'll have a team of exceptions. I'm talking about size. I borrowed that from Tom Landry."

On Draft Day, Wolf wanted everything to go smoothly for the Packers. He didn't want anyone jumping or pounding on tables during the Draft, and no one ever did under Wolf because he made it crystal clear, "If somebody wants to do that they'd get escorted out of the room." As much as they had their process, though, they still had natural emotions at times. "We were going with the Board. That doesn't mean that you don't get caught up in a situation, like I had a chance in '96, we were one pick away from Ray Lewis. We were talking to Ray Lewis. We were talking to Ray Lewis' agent. Our guy was standing at the podium with Ray Lewis' name on the card to hand in, and darn it, Baltimore did take him. Yeah, so, that's part of it."

It's little moments like that which ultimately change the course of history. Baltimore would go on to win two Super Bowls with Ray Lewis leading the way. But what if they hadn't taken him and he landed in Green Bay? Would they have won more Super Bowls in Green Bay? Would the Ravens have become a mainstay in the AFC playoffs for the next decade plus still? There is no way of telling, but it's proof of how much the NFL Draft matters for all parties involved.

Speaking of moments that would alter history for both a franchise and a future Pro Football Hall of Fame player, Ron Wolf was hired and arrived in Green Bay sometime after Thanksgiving in 1991 to become their general manager after previously working for the New York Jets. As every general manager knows, if you want any chance of succeeding, you must have a foundational first Draft to set the tone for the entire franchise. Wolf and the Packers held the nineteenth pick in the first round of the 1992 NFL Draft and Wolf went on to make a splash not many first-time general managers would have the guts to make.

"I've been working, the year before in 1991, with the New York Jets and I scouted (Brett) Favre at Southern Mississippi and then in the East-West (Shrine) Game. And I was convinced, I was sitting there with Dick Steinberg who was the general manager of the Jets, and we were at the East-West (Shrine) Game and we were talking that Brett Favre was the best player in the Draft, and I said, 'No question about that.' With the Jets, he was our first player on the Board. Now the Jets had a different Board than we had with the Packers, but he was still the first player on the Board. Fortunately for me, the Jets didn't have a first-round pick. They used a supplemental draft pick on Rod Moore. So, the whole time we're trying to work a deal to move up to get Favre because he's still there as we start the second round and is one pick away from us when Atlanta picks him. So, my first day on the job (with the Packers), the first game

I went to in '91 was in December in Atlanta, Fulton County Stadium, and obviously we're playing the Atlanta Falcons. I worked with Kenny Herock for a long time in Oakland and he was a player with the Raiders, became a scout with the Raiders, and all that. He comes up to me at a press box and says, 'If you want to see Brett Favre throw, you better go down now because once the team comes out, they won't let him take part in the workout.' So, I knew right away that I had an opportunity to get the guy that I thought was the best player in the Draft in '91. I sat with Bob Harlan and started talking to him about that and he said, 'That's good, you can bring it up to the executive committee on Tuesday. We'll meet Tuesday in Green Bay after the game. You can bring it up and talk to them about it.' Which I did. I would have loved to have been a fly on the wall because I'm sure after I got done and left the room, those guys really went after Harlan saying, 'You hired some cuckoo from New York!' Here's a guy couldn't even make the team picture, that's what they thought of him in Atlanta. Obviously, it still worked out. I was in the game thirty-eight years and he's the best player I ever was around."

What Wolf accomplished in his time with the Green Bay Packers is nothing short of outstanding. He brought championship football back to "Titletown," and he did it in impressive and bold fashion. Nothing can show how great of a system Wolf had like the following. "I was very fortunate in being able to assemble a really competent staff in Green Bay. Six of those guys went on to become general managers, two of them led their teams to winning Super Bowls, and one guy built a Super Bowl team, so, put it like this, I had a lot of help."

If that isn't enough of a legacy for Wolf, his own son, Eliot, has been working in the NFL on the personnel side since 2004. Wolf's legacy is much more than a championship roster in Green Bay; it's the success of all those that have learned the right way to go about this very process from him.

SECTION III

THE COACHES

N FL COACHES HAVE a unique influence on the NFL Draft because while they are the ones who will coach the players selected, they also cannot focus on the Draft much, if at all, until their own season is over. Because of that, you will find that there is more variety to how coaches work during the pre-Draft period.

In this section, you will find stories from three gentlemen who would all become NFL head coaches across four different franchises, including one who led his team to a Super Bowl championship. The coach who won the Super Bowl had a great situation with a great working relationship with his scouting department year in and year out. The one who was the head coach for multiple franchises had two polar-opposite experiences in those places. The other head coach actually found out exactly what he would do differently if given the opportunity again. It's incredibly informative to hear the many different experiences a coach can have throughout the Draft process.

Each head coach had different experiences, so this chapter will share insights about how much film they actually watch, whether or not they have decision making power with selections, and the role assistant coaches played during the process. When it comes down to it, the importance of a great general manager and scouting department was evident when talking to these three. They wouldn't use that to pit any sort of blame in situations necessarily, but rather as a key point you will pick up as a reader in both positive and negative circumstances. The fact that head coaches enter the process later than everyone else forces them to have a level of trust that the scouting department has done their due diligence. Whether they watch full games, ten-play clips, a lot of prospects, or only targeted prospects, it all starts with the recommendations and research done by the scouts.

These coaches first viewed the Draft as assistants and then became head coaches with different franchises. They then had to learn how a brand-new scouting department handled the Draft period. For some, it was a smooth transition similar to where they came from, but you will learn here that is not always the case, and sometimes you can go from great to poor real fast.

While each situation was unique, I did find that coaches all had similar opinions when giving their take on which prospects they preferred: they typically looked for guys they could coach and who loved football. For scouting departments, it's easy to get lost in measurables and traits, but for coaches there is still the understanding that these prospects will quickly turn into players on your team and ultimately need to be guys they can coach. How much weight their opinions carry is one of many answers you will find in this section.

BILL COWHER
Drafting Character

E VERYONE WHO KNOWS football, knows Bill Cowher—the man who roamed the Pittsburgh Steelers'
sideline for fifteen years as their head coach. The
Steelers players during his time weren't the only ones who
had a presence on gameday. Cowher had the size at 6-foot-
3, the scowl with the caricature jaw, and the animation and
competitive fire that could rival any player he coached and
any coach the game has ever seen. What a lot of people don't
know is how Bill Cowher got the title of "Coach Cowher" in
the first place.

Cowher, a linebacker out of North Carolina State University (NC State), went undrafted in 1979, but signed as
a free agent with the Philadelphia Eagles. While Cowher
made it to the very end of training camp and preseason, he
was eventually cut. He headed back to NC State to become

a graduate assistant with the football team as he finished his final semester of school and got his first introduction into coaching. This is not the classic start to a legendary coaching career that many may have expected, however. Cowher got his degree and wanted to give playing the game he was coaching one more try.

Bill Cowher signed as a street free agent with the Cleveland Browns in 1980 where he spent two seasons. He received a $1,000 signing bonus, which after taxes came out to a whopping $644. It wasn't about the money to Cowher, though. After two years in Cleveland, Cowher would wrap up his playing career back in Philadelphia for another two seasons. Understanding that he could likely hang on a few more years as a player, but still knowing he would be a guy fighting and clawing for a final roster spot each year, Cowher considered a new offer from a former coach he had in Cleveland. Marty Schottenheimer took over as the head coach of the Cleveland Browns in 1984 after previously being the defensive coordinator where he coached a young Bill Cowher. Knowing Cowher's make up as a player and leader, Schottenheimer called Cowher to gauge his interest in becoming a special teams coach for the Browns. He started by asking Cowher how much he was set to make as a player the following year if he kept playing. Schottenheimer's response is as straight as an arrow.

"(Cowher) said, 'About $150,000' and (Schottenheimer) said, 'Well, you're going to work three times as much and make three times as less. I'll give you $50,000,'" Cowher recalled. Not much of a sales pitch, but if you know Cowher, he appreciated the honesty. At the age of twenty-eight Cowher left the NFL as a player but remained in the league as a coach.

While Cowher would become the infamous head coach of the Pittsburgh Steelers in 1992, he had plenty of experience as a coach for the NFL Draft from his time spent as an assistant coach.

"I had seven years as an assistant in the National Football League, so I watched as an assistant what the Drafts consisted of and what your role was as an assistant coach. In other words, I would go in there, particularly as a special teams coach, I would go in there when they were talking about the kickers, and you had the scouts, and you had the people that were putting together grades and talking about the strengths and weaknesses. I became a secondary coach (and) I was doing the same thing. Then we went to Kansas City, and I was a linebackers coach and defensive coordinator, so I would go into a lot of these meetings. I wouldn't sit there at the Combine and talk to a lot of the players. I would come in with Marty whenever my position was being interviewed."

The experience of being with the head coach and general manager during these interviews and other moments would be invaluable to Cowher because he was able to see everything that went into the Draft from the organization standpoint. Cowher also would see what went into Draft Day itself, and the making and importance of having a Board to work off. "There's a lot of different ways of doing it (the Board), and pretty much you're grading each position, and then you're prioritizing. You're putting the talent you have, (marked) one through five of each position, but then number one at one position, may be equal to the value of number three at another position. So, you're having a horizontal Board and a vertical Board, sort of speak, and people do it differently," Cowher explained.

When Cowher first took over in Pittsburgh in 1992, free agency wasn't what it is today. The organizations knew that if they drafted the right guys for their football team, they would have them for the long haul. It made it easier for them to draft because they not only knew where they need to get better for the upcoming season, but they had a much better idea of who will be around still a few years down the line. Free agency would change all that.

"There's a lot more factors that got involved with that, and it was more of a case of having to value the player, but also you have to look at your football team and say where does that player fit? I may only have this guy for four years, so now you're almost thinking like a college coach." Cowher continued to discuss how the conversations concerning when and how to sign these players would become critical.

Not only did you now have to have real conversations on when to sign your own players, you also had the opportunity to look around the league and sign other free agents yourself. It really made teams start to evaluate the big picture because it was now possible to lose more of your key players. You had to decide how to best fill your needs, whether in free agency or the Draft. For Cowher, he felt for a while that they ended up training players for other teams. They would come in, get developed and trained in their system, only to leave as they entered their prime years as a football player. In terms of the Draft, it changed how you might go about making your Board due to the needs you didn't address in free agency. As Cowher said, "Talent and need had to be balanced delicately and I think it was also very subjective each year." The type of players placed on their Board, though, were graded on more than just their talent alone.

"There's a lot of different ways of doing it. You put a grade on talent. You put a grade on character. You put a grade on potential. You're looking at is this guy as good as he can be? Can this guy get better? Does this guy love football? You're talking to all the trainers. You're talking to all the coaches. You sit there and talk to every player. One of the questions I used to ask at the Combine was, 'If you had some of the worst news in the world that was given to you, who's the first person you call? If you just won the lottery, who's the first person you would call?' So, you find out where these guys are, who's instrumental in their lives. I just I wanted to know their make-up. Who they were as people because to me, I'm not just coaching a player, I'm coaching a person and I need to know that person. The quality (of) the character was important, but also you recognize some of these guys (growing up), they weren't given the opportunity to mature. I saw guys become men right before my eyes because all of a sudden now they had freedom, you've got money in your pocket. It's not like in college where everything is structured. You go to the meal hall, you're told what to do, and everything is there. Now you're not being told what to do and is this guy capable of handling that kind of responsibility? You're constantly evaluating these people trying to get to know them as people, players, and it just became a part of the grades that we put on things."

The big question when it comes to the Draft for coaches is how much time do they actually get to spend on studying the prospects? With the Draft typically falling at the end of April or early May, these coaches, specifically those coaching deep into the playoffs like Cowher was during his career, don't have a lot of time to catch up on every play of every prospect. The understanding here is that each coach, general manager, and organization would handle this in different ways. For Cowher, as soon as the season was over, he would talk to the general manager to sense where they were looking based on who could be around at their draft position that year, so he knew who to dial in on when he went to the NFL Scouting Combine. There was one base rule he wanted to follow. He always wanted the Steelers to come out of Round 3 with a lineman, a playmaker at either running back or wide receiver, and a defensive back. The order in which those positions went in the first three rounds was dependent on the value of the player available, but after three rounds, he wanted a guy in each of those position groups if possible.

Cowher spoke to the general manager about the needs they felt should be addressed. Some could be handled in free agency, though Cowher admitted Pittsburgh was never a huge player for big-money free agents during his time there.Even today there are organizations who aren't nearly as aggressive in free agency as others. They did, however, have a few big additions that they did not originally draft, including the NFL's eighth all-time leading rusher, Jerome Bettis. Bettis, a product of the University of Notre Dame, was selected by the Los Angeles Rams with the tenth overall pick in the first round of the 1992 NFL Draft. As a rookie, Bettis ran for 1,429 yards and made 1st Team All-Pro honors. In his second season his production went down to 1,025 rushing yards on only 3.2 yard per carry. Finally, in 1995, Bettis ran for only 637 yards for the Rams and the Steelers knew that he had more in the tank and traded for the young, bruising running back. The reason Bettis made sense for Pittsburgh was because they were going to have to take a running back in the upcoming Draft anyway, why not use picks on a known product?

Once Cowher had the top targets for the Steelers, he would make sure to watch a game or two to give himself a better idea of the player before they got to the NFL Scouting Combine interviews. Once that was over and the position coaches began to further break down prospect film, Cowher would assign them a task. "I used to ask them to put together a ten-play Cliff Notes with this player. And I want to see the good and I also want to see some of the concerns that we may have, because we don't get a highlight film and make someone look like an All-American. I don't want to see a freaking highlight film," Cowher emphasized while saying they didn't want the opposite either. "I had a guy like Russ Grimm (offensive line coach). If Russ didn't like a guy, he'd bring it in, he'd show the ten worst plays that the guy ever probably had," Cowher laughed.

Cowher knew he had to sort through and understand that there were guys certain people would just like more and guys certain people would like less. He learned to take it with a grain of salt and understand opinions were involved, which is why he would sit there and write down four or five different reports to find the common denominators on a guy. Once Cowher and their staff finished up the ten-play reels, they started comparing prospects. During this part of the process was when they really started digging into the stuff that wouldn't always show up on tape. They would have more conversations about character. They would talk about injury history and consult with doctors. They also would speak to a player's college coaches, and Cowher spoke about how the amount of weight each coach's opinion carried would vary. "It becomes very subjective. You talked to Nick (Saban), who's been in the National Football League, so he can give you a reference (because) he gets it, because he's coached in the National Football League." Cowher explained they all aren't like Saban.

> "You take it with a grain of salt. You see one thing. You hear from them. They're not going to throw anybody under the bus, but my question is 'Can you depend on him? Can you count on him? What's he like in a locker room? Was he a leader for you? If you want to get the pulse of your team, can you talk to this guy? Does this guy give you the pulse of this team? Is he your leader? Is he the best worker? Have you ever had any issues with his family? Is there anything else that comes with him that we may not be aware of?' It's just gathering information."

Cowher knew that the player reflected the coach's program, so the only real negative stuff you would get from them is if it was really bad and in the public eye. Part of the issue in Cowher's eyes was that most of these coaches never coached in the NFL. They only viewed these players as a college player, but it's a different game in the pros. "I brought more college coaches on my staffs and a lot of them just never fit in because they tell kids what to do. If the kid doesn't listen to them, he's a bad kid because they shouldn't even question it. In college, you tell the kid what to do and the kid's supposed to do it and most of the times they will. You come to the pros, you tell him what to do the kid's going to say, 'Why?' and you can't be offended by that," Cowher explained.

Eventually, using all the variables above, they would put a grade on a player and start forming the Board. As the Draft got closer and free agency was over, they really focused on watching more film and dialing in on who they expected to be available when they were picking and what needs needed to be filled for their football team. In 2004, while Cowher was eying University of Arkansas offensive lineman Shawn Andrews for their first pick, as the Draft got closer, he felt there was a chance Miami University quarterback Ben Roethlisberger just might be available. In case that happened, Cowher went back and watched every game of Roethlisberger's senior season. Cowher came away impressed, and his information was spot on as Roethlisberger would be available for the Steelers with the eleventh pick in the first round. Andrews would go five picks later to the Philadelphia Eagles.

As expected, it was not uncommon that people of influence would disagree on who they should pick. In Pittsburgh during Cowher's reign, the Steelers' owner at the time, Mr.

Dan Rooney, didn't have any clauses in anyone's contract that gave them final say in a dispute like this. If you had a dispute and couldn't come to an agreement, Mr. Rooney would simply tell them they better get back in there and work it out. Cowher felt that set-up provided a healthy give and take for the Steelers.

It is hard to find a team that drafts better than the Pittsburgh Steelers do consistently, and that was evident especially in the Cowher-era. Cowher put an emphasis on drafting players that loved football, had a blue-collar work ethic, and had high character. With many players that fit that mold, Cowher noted a few of his favorite gems and Draft picks.

"That's a good one [referring to Hines Ward]. Another guy along the same lines that I really just got to like him a lot, because we were doing interviews at the Combine (and) he just brought his head in, it was Antwan Randle El. I said, 'Let's interview Antwan.' Antwan also played for Bobby Knight, so he was a basketball player, too, at Indiana. He was a quarterback there, but then he played in the Senior Bowl (and) they put him at receiver, so he played one game as a receiver in the slot. When you get around this guy, there was just a bubbliness about him. He was just a good guy. Just

like a fun guy who had all this energy and the smile
and this confidence about him."

Cowher loved the fact that Randle El was tough, having played
without a ligament in his knee since high school, according
to Cowher. He was a do-it-all star in college, and it turns out
that is exactly what he was in NFL, too. Cowher also was very
proud of being able to identify guys that fit their identity such
as Mike Vrabel and Chad Brown, who played with their hands
in the dirt in college but were drafted to be stand-up outside
linebackers for the Steelers 3-4 defense. While the role of a 4-3
defensive end and a 3-4 outside linebacker have similarities,
there are enough differences, specifically in their ability to
rush the passer from a two-point stance, that it takes a keen
eye and great coaching to identify the correct players who can
make the transition. Then there were guys like Troy Polamalu
and Alan Faneca, two Pro Football Hall of Famers, who were
just special the moment they laid eyes on them. They became
a reflection of the team. Some guys turned out to be too much
of a distraction for Cowher's liking, as well, not that he wanted
a team full of church mice either.

"When they crossed the line, my job was to pull them
back. I wanted our football team to walk as close to

that line as possible. I want them to be on the verge of being cocky, confident, play the game that when you go out there, you're the best one on the field and I'll pull you back when I think that you did something that disrespects the game, that disrespects the opponent, that disrespects your teammates. We tried to build a culture like that where it was respectful, but it was confident, and we played together and we just had a brashness about us that quite frankly I was trying to cultivate."

What helped Cowher relate to his players was his own playing experience. Players knew he had been through it himself as a player, which helps gain the respect of the locker room. When your head coach has been there and loves the game as much or more than you do, the credibility skyrockets.

Just how did Cowher handle NFL players for all those years coaching, dealing with contracts and complaining at times? He had a little help in a frame from his past: his 1980 signing bonus from the Cleveland Browns. "I got that frame hung out in my office all those years of coaching. When guys came in here bullsh*t about not getting enough signing bonus, I said 'Let me just take you over here to what I got when I played.' It's like, it really wasn't about how much money I made because I love the game."

Something that is evident in the NFL is that a team often takes on the identity and personality of their head coach. In Pittsburgh during Cowher's reign there was no question that his teams did just that—playing with the toughness, grit, and love of the game that Cowher is made of. You see it in today's NFL with cross-characteristics of teams and their head coaches. The New England Patriots under Bill Belichick are known for being incredibly detailed, prepared, and disciplined. The similarities are uncanny and not a coincidence. The Los Angeles Rams are creative, ahead of the curve, and play with incredible juice, which are traits that head coach Sean McVay can't help but to display himself. Finally, John Harbaugh gives his team incredible confidence in their abilities and proves he trusts them in many scenarios, which in turn gives the team confidence and trust in their head coach. It's a reason why he is considered one the best "player coaches" in the NFL. To do this the right way, however, it starts with the Draft and with the players you bring into your program. If you want those players to take on the personality of their head coach, it helps if they already have the football DNA and traits the coach is looking for. That's why the communication process is so vital and why Cowher believed in the pre-Draft process so much. There is no question that the Pro Football Hall of Famer succeeded in every aspect as a head coach, including during the months where they weren't even playing games.

STEVE MARIUCCI
Building Trust

"I'M THE QUARTERBACK coach of the Green Bay Packers and Ron Wolf walks into my office and he gives me a piece of paper and he says, 'Evaluate this guy. Tell me what you think.' He puts a piece of paper out. It's Brett Favre, Atlanta Falcons." This was Steve Mariucci's first job in the National Football League. Ron Wolf had just arrived as the new general manager for the Green Bay Packers, and they were approaching their first NFL Draft in 1992. Mariucci got the assignment and went to work. However, because he had just come from coaching in the college ranks and Favre barely played in Atlanta as a rookie, Mariucci had to dig into Favre's old college film at Southern Mississippi.

"I had to go back and look at Southern Miss film, and I saw a strongarmed quarterback—gunslinger—that was an excitable guy. He would go jumping around all over the place after a touchdown pass or he hyperventilated one time and was under the bench and they had to find him because he kind of passed out. I mean he's a wild and crazy guy that everybody loved down at Southern Miss. They beat Alabama and all that stuff. I wrote a report up after watching some college film and just a few plays from the Atlanta Falcons and Ron goes, 'Well, what do you think?' And I go, 'Well, it's right there. He's got a strong arm and he's a gunslinger. He takes chances. He's raw. He looks like a tough guy. He's emotional that's for sure.' He goes, 'Okay, fine, that's all I want to know from you.' So, like two days later he trades for him!"

Mariucci was surprised after Wolf made the move so quickly. He admits he's not sure if Wolf went through that with him to humor him or if he just wanted him to feel a part of the evaluation, but he said the staff had to put their trust in Wolf.

"We trade for the guy. I don't know all that much about (Favre). I don't think the Packer fans knew much about him. So, we had to just trust Ron Wolf. We were a new staff—me and Andy Reid and Jon Gruden and Dick Jauron and Ray Rhodes and Sherm Lewis—all a young bunch of guys. So, when I was there, we were working. We did this trade and everything, but I had to leave and go home because my wife was still living in California, my kid's going to school, and so I had to go home and get some new clothes and see them."

From his memory, Mariucci believes that was the time when head coach Mike Holmgren sent most of the staff away for a quick break. During that time, they brought Favre into Green Bay for the first time, before he headed back to Mississippi for the remainder of his time off until he had to report back to Green Bay for the offseason. Mariucci was out in California, and up to this point, he had still never spoken to Favre. "I'm home and the phone rings. No cell phones yet, there's the phone landline, and the guy on the phone goes, 'Is Coach (Mar-oochi) there?' I go, 'This is he. Who's this?' (The guy answers), 'Brett.' I go, 'Brett who? Oh, Brett Favre! Hi Brett, how are you doing? Hey, congratulations!' He goes, 'Thank you.'"

Next, Mariucci will encounter one of the most bizarre first meetings a coach has ever and will ever have with his new quarterback.

"[Favre] goes, 'Well, I only have one phone call, so I thought I'd give you a call' and I looked at the phone like 'What? One phone call? What are you talking about?' He goes, 'Well, you got to promise you're not going to say anything to anybody.' This is the first time I ever talked to Brett Favre. He's in jail! This is how we met, okay? I didn't go recruit him. I didn't go work him out. I don't know Brett Favre. Our first conversation he's in jail. He gets one phone call, and he calls me! He goes, 'Well, thought I'd better call you because I only get one phone call.' I go, 'You're in jail, what the heck?!' I said, 'First of all, why didn't you call Mike Holmgren?' He goes, 'Oh, he'd kill me' and I go, 'Well, why didn't you call Ron Wolf?' Then he goes, 'Oh, he'd really kill me' and I go, 'Oh, so you're going to call me, right?!' "

Mariucci said he kind of liked that Favre called him and told him the truth. He asked Favre what happened, and Favre explained he was out at the bar in Hattiesburg, MS with his siblings and friends shooting pool when someone bumped into his brother who then bumped his sister and that started a bar fight, which ended with a group going to jail. Mariucci's immediate reaction was, "Oh my God, this is our quarterback."

Favre wasn't too concerned about it, believe it or not, he just felt someone should know in case it somehow got out. Remember, this is before the days of social media and Favre wasn't even in Green Bay at the time. He was comfortable knowing it won't turn into anything, he just wanted to get out in front of it just in case it did. However, letting the Packers know was one thing. Letting anyone else in the Packers organization know was something Favre begged Mariucci not to do.

> "[Favre] said, 'You got to just promise me you won't tell Mike or Ron, okay? Promise me.' Mariucci knew he was put in a tough spot as a first-year quarterback coach with his new quarterback. Mariucci decided he believed Favre telling him it wasn't a big deal and ultimately didn't believe it was anything concerning about his character. "So I go, 'Alright, I'll make you deal' — We're making deals in our first conversation! — 'You promise this crap is never going to happen again, and I can keep it a secret. It can be yours and mine. But, if this stuff happens again, now they're going to know immediately that you are crazy.'"

Mariucci couldn't help but to laugh while sharing the story. He understands how unbelievable of a first encounter it is for an NFL coach with his new quarterback. Do you want to know the best part? Mariucci kept that secret for Favre's entire playing career. He has told it since Favre has retired, but he made sure to be good to his word during Favre's career, and he believes that was the best thing that could have happened. "He learned that my word was good. He learned to trust me. He learned that I had his back. To this day I have his back and he probably has my back. It was kind of a player-coach thing."

Welcome to the NFL Draft, Steve Mariucci! Your team used their first-round pick on a player that you, one way or another, helped endorse on film, only to have him put you between a rock and hard place before ever meeting. The first player Mariucci ever "drafted" (in a way) for his position group, he met while the player was in jail.

Mariucci had experiences like that from his time as an assistant coach in the NFL, but he has also been a head coach in two different spots with the San Francisco 49ers and the Detroit Lions. Mariucci made a point to clarify that he can only speak from his experiences and is not speaking for other organizations or philosophies.

Mariucci said the scouts were there year-round to evaluate. They evaluated every day unless they were on a vacation. And they went over every kid on the Board, which Mariucci said could be in the neighborhood of 1,100 prospects or more.

From his experience, the coaches didn't have year-round Draft responsibilities, specifically during the season. They would naturally watch some big games during the college football season on a Saturday and know the top quarterbacks and Heisman candidates but would not do any evaluations at that time.

"As soon as your season is over with, whether you're done after your regular season or your playoffs, the first thing that most coaches are going to do is take a week and send their players off, meet with their players, say goodbye, and then do a self-scout for a week. It's a process where you're evaluating not only your players and ranking them, you're evaluating your scheme, your red zone package, your protections, your short yardage and goal line, all that. So, you do a thorough self-scout, and the other thing is you're doing a self-scout on your players. I still have them right here in my office. Our evaluations of our team and their grades by the coach and by the coordinator and by the head coach."

Mariucci and the coaching staff would do those reports and give them to the general manager. These reports helped determine the guys they were counting on and who the coaches absolutely loved. In the end, the general manager used these along with their salary and cap hits to determine who they would target to keep on their own team. This would help determine who they needed to target in the Draft. The example Mariucci used was if they were going to lose Jerry Rice, and Terrell Owens was due for a pay day, then they would have to draft a wide receiver. They would literally put that on their depth chart on the Board in their Draft room. They would also not make a rash decision just because they had a player graded high. "Need" was still a big part of the process. "If there's a great tight end out there, let's say there's a freaking stud tight end like Kyle Pitts in (the 2021) Draft who was a top ten player in the Draft, but I got Tony Gonzalez on the team. We're not going to draft Kyle Pitts," he explained. "We might have him evaluated and ranked way the hell up on top, but our needs don't say we need that guy. If we're going to get a tight end, it'll be a backup. It might be a blocking tight end that you can find in the late rounds."

Mariucci's staff would all evaluate prospects at their position during that time before Draft Day. What is eye-opening about this process is how the coaches would evaluate a lot of players. Mariucci said his staff would watch at least everyone that was invited to the NFL Scouting Combine, at the minimum, even if they had no plans on drafting that position. These evaluations would be a go-to source of information when there were injuries in camp, someone was needed for the practice squad, or they simply wanted to make a run at a free agent down the road. Mariucci and the staff used the time to evaluate not just for the current Draft, but for days, weeks, and sometimes even years later. This went back to Mariucci's days under Ron Wolf in Green Bay, when he had to evaluate quarterbacks annually. Yes, quarterbacks, on a depth chart where Brett Favre was QB1. They would spend a mid-round draft pick on guys like Ty Detmer and Mark Brunell because they were cheaper. They were very honest and told them they were coming in to be Favre's backup, something Green Bay continued to do even after Mariucci was gone by bringing in the likes of Matt Hasselbeck. Mariucci took this responsibility seriously. "Go to the school (and) spend the whole day with the kid. Get him on the board, get him on the field, work him out, talk to coaches, secretaries, strength coaches, defensive coaches." Mariucci continued, "Really dig deep, take him to dinner, to lunch, see if he eats with a knife and a fork. I mean, just everything. You try to do the best you can with getting to know the kid on and off the field."

Mariucci was in a War Room fourteen different times for Draft Day. While the general managers, especially Ron Wolf, worked off the Board, everyone was never in one-hundred percent agreement and Wolf allowed for conversation after the first few rounds if he felt it was needed.

"Ron is as good as they get and so here's where the discussions came. The discussions came if it could be a third or fourth or fifth rounder and there's a lot of guys on the Board that you could take here and it's going to be our turn in four more picks. You're looking at the Board and there will be times that Ron will turn his head and look and go, 'Alright, let's talk about those four guys.' It could be a linebacker, a receiver, a running back, and a defensive tackle. He would have the scout and the coach, not politic for those guys, but talk about him and about 'Can we do without him? Do we have to get him right now? How much will he play? How badly do we need this kid?' and there's discussion. That's why everyone was sitting in there to have discussion if need be. When you have discussion, I learned that, hey, the receiver coach always wants the receiver, and the running back coach always wants the runner, and the defensive line coach always wants the fat guy with the three-point stance. That's where one person has to make a decision and that's going to be a strong personnel guy like Ron Wolf."

On top of film, the conversation and evaluations also included other factors, such as character, coachability, medical history, and personality fit. Scouts and coaches could sometimes have different opinions on that. For instance, the coach may prefer a prospect who is graded a little lower but has zero-character issues and is extremely coachable.

After spending his first two stints in the NFL with two of the most well-run organizations in league history, Mariucci headed off to become the head coach of the Detroit Lions before the 2003 NFL Draft. This was a much different experience for Mariucci because his first order of business was to hire a coaching staff, which took some time. He did retain a few coaches who knew the players, which was to Mariucci's benefit because he didn't know "these Lions" all that well. Mariucci still recalls his Wizard of Oz type "We're not in San Francisco anymore" moment when he first went into the Lions' War Room. "I walked into it, and I looked at the Board and it was embarrassing. The magnetic cards were all haphazard and written in different magic markers, and some had big magnets and some (were) weird and some were different sizes, and it was like, 'Where am I?' I couldn't believe how far behind that scouting department was with the rest of the league," Mariucci remembered. "The first thing we had to do is reorganize how we are going to put players' names up on a Board and organize the information on these Boards."

Growing up in the Draft School of John McVay in San Francisco and Ron Wolf in Green Bay, Mariucci was used to a well-oiled machine this time of year. The first step was to integrate some of what each had taught Mariucci into Detroit's way of doing things. Mariucci didn't blame anyone in the scouting department; it was something that just wasn't as good as it needed to be by any stretch of the imagination.

Mariucci's experiences were all different and it's those experiences that make him so knowledgeable and valuable to this day on NFL Network as an analyst. Mariucci has experienced as much as one could in his fourteen seasons as an NFL coach. The common theme throughout his experience was the importance of building trust. Whether it was Ron Wolf trusting his evaluation of Favre, keeping a secret right off the bat for Favre, or working his tail off in Detroit to build trust that would allow him to reorganize the way the Board was made. Mariucci used his good word and experience to build trust across every relationship he had in the NFL.

MIKE SINGLETARY
Lessons Learned

MIKE SINGLETARY TOOK his legendary passion as a Pro Football Hall of Fame linebacker and went into coaching. He had a very successful start to his NFL coaching career by mentoring a future Pro Football Hall of Fame linebacker, Ray Lewis, as the Baltimore Ravens linebackers coach from 2003-2004. In 2005, Singletary joined the San Francisco 49ers coaching staff and ultimately, became the team's interim head coach during the 2008 season after Mike Nolan was fired. Singletary helped lead the 49ers to a 5-4 record the remainder of the season, which was good enough to get the 'interim' title removed and make Singletary the permanent head coach starting in 2009. Singletary was the head coach of the 49ers through the 2010 season and finished his head coaching career with a 18-22 record.

When it came to the NFL Draft, Singletary knew there were some areas that he had supreme knowledge in, and others on which he could improve.

"One of the things that I know very well is talent, and more so than talent is heart. I don't need a guy that was All-American in college. I don't need it. Show me the guy that busts his tail on every play. The problem that I had the second year I was head coach is I really had to rely on my assistants, and I asked a couple of guys questions about this player, that player, and I leaned on them more so than scouts, which was a mistake. It was a mistake because what I should have been doing is really looking at film myself, but I trusted a couple of coaches and I asked them, 'What do you think about this guy? He's a big guy. He can run and do this and do that.' The coach said, 'Coach, this guy can play! He just hasn't been coached, that's all.' That's music to my ears. We got a guy that's got a (high) ceiling, can run, can do this, can do that. To make a long story short, he was a bad pick, but that will forever be somebody that I put my name on. I'm going to fall on the sword for this guy because my coach said, 'This is the guy. He can play.'"

Singletary learned the importance of placing his trust in the right people. Although he may never get the opportunity to do-over as a head coach in the National Football League, that still doesn't stop him from thinking about what he would do differently if given the chance, though:

> "If I had to it all over again, I would be in that room with that projector with that video and I'm looking at every player and I'm going to put my name on him. I'm going to fall on the sword for him, but I'm not going to take anybody's words that this guy is 'the guy.' I'm going to interview him. I'm going to talk to him. I'm going to go to their hometown. I'm going to talk to coaches. The thing that I learned is that if I'm going to coach a guy, now certainly the scouts are important and all those things, but if I'm going to coach a guy and I know what system I'm going to play, I want that guy to know that I'm going to coach him like I would coach to my son. I'm going to give him all of me. If he's got a problem, I want to know what it is and nine times out of ten I would know that he has a problem because I know his history."

Singletary continued to say that he simply didn't know what he didn't know. He went from having no coaching experience to becoming an NFL head coach within six years. Even though it all fell apart in his second season as the permanent head coach, he still views it as a tremendous experience. If he could do it all over, he never trust the scouts solely, but would be in the room with them debating prospects to be able to come to the best possible decisions for the organization.

When talking with Singletary, it's clear he still has a passion for the game of football and coaching. When he spoke about what he would do differently, it didn't come across as a guy looking at his past, but rather a guy planning for his future. It certainly begged the question: is Mike Singletary planning to coach in the NFL again?

"I have an agent, but I just said, 'Lord I'm turning this over to you,' because it's amazing you can get a head coaching job when you don't know anything, but then you can't get one when you sacrifice to learn everything. For me it's a tough thing, that's why you don't see guys that have played the game coaching the game, particularly a Hall of Famer, because coaches just don't really know how to treat you. They don't know how to respond. Particularly with me because I'm a leader a lot of guys gravitated to me and so I tried to stay out of the way. Most people just said, 'Mike, just be quiet. Mike just stay back, just hide,' but that's really difficult for me to do because I'm a leader and when I see things I speak. I don't want to speak, but I do. I know when something is not right. I know when a player is out of line, and I know when a coach is out of line. Just being somewhere, just being a figurehead that's not it. That would be an insult to all the people that had a place in my life. If I'm there I need to be there for a reason, and if it's not to win, then I don't need to be there, I need to be doing something else."

Mike Singletary is a leader of men who learned from his past. It is commendable to see someone so successful be able to admit areas that would need improvement if given an opportunity again. If that opportunity arose to be a head coach of an NFL franchise again, I have no doubt that players would gravitate to him and play hard for him once again. The franchise would instantly improve their Draft process too, because Singletary will make the needed adjustments to help bring in the players that he knows he can coach. Understanding talent and knowing how to acquire the talent are two different concepts, but now Singletary has a grasp on the latter one as well. I am not sure if we will ever see Singletary get this opportunity again, but I will certainly be rooting for it to happen and rooting for Coach Singletary when and if it does.

SECTION IV

THE

PLAYERS

N O GROUP OF people's lives change more during the NFL Draft than the players themselves. For better or for worse, the players have a lifechanging weekend. Due to the media and even the players themselves sharing bits and pieces of their own Draft stories, they are the one angle in this book that fans have had the most insight into. There are still some topics that the average fan has no idea about and truths that even the diehards likely don't understand. They are also the only ones in this book who only go through the Draft process one time, so a wider net was cast for this section. In this section, stories are uncovered that will resolve some unanswered questions.

Here you will read the Draft stories from ten players who went through the NFL Draft process. As of the completion of the 2021-2022 season, those ten players have combined to produce sixty-one Pro Bowls, six Super Bowl wins, eight NFL MVPs, and six current Pro Football Hall of Fame memberships. Of the ten players, three were drafted in the first round, two in the second round, one in the fourth round, one in the sixth round, one in the ninth round, one went undrafted, and one went in the NFL's Supplemental Draft. It's safe to say there is a vast landscape of experiences based on where they were or were not selected.

Given the opportunity to pull back the curtain on all ten of their Draft experiences, I knew I needed to ask the questions that truly were the most unknown to fans. Do players have any idea who will take them on Draft Day? Did they have a lot of communication with the team that selected them prior to the Draft? What were their conversations with teams like prior to the Draft? Were there any unique workout stories? Were there any medical reasons that were hiccups in their Draft stock? Did they have any plans besides football if the Draft didn't go as they hoped? Were there any deemed "weaknesses" as a prospect that were later proven wrong in their careers? Were they happy where they were drafted, or was it a bittersweet moment based on the organization or location?

These questions needed to be answered because it doesn't always—in fact it rarely—seems to go as expected. There seems to be a general assumption that a player is picked by a team that had a lot of conversations with him, he is unbelievably happy to go there, and all is right with the world. Based on the stories from the ten players above, you will learn that is often far from the truth. There may not be a lot of shock per say for the players because they likely have a good agent who has informed them with some likely possibilities for both

Draft position and team as we learned in the Agent section before. However, there are always a few surprises that will shake up a Draft Board and send a player's future into the great unknown. That's what makes the Draft great and puts fans on the edge of their seats in excitement. Yet, for players, it's moments like those that have a ripple effect and will put knots in their stomachs and doubts in their heads.

In the end, my favorite part of talking with each of these men was the pride and joy I could feel as each told his story. Many went on to Pro Football Hall of Fame careers and great lives after football, but I could still hear the very excitement and suspense that I'm sure they experienced when they went through the Draft process. The Draft is a lifechanging experience for everyone, but for the players one day will impact the rest of their lives both on and off the football field.

BENNIE BLADES
Bad Boys for Life

N THE 1980S, the University of Miami, better known as "The U," was basically another NFL team. From the talent, the scenery, the swagger, and the way they played football, players that came from "The U" were as ready for the NFL as an NFL prospect could be. Star safety Bennie Blades was at the forefront of those Miami teams and his play epitomized everything that Miami was about. "Coming from Miami at that time, we were larger than the Miami Dolphins. It was a rock star atmosphere. So, getting ready for the Draft most of us such as myself (and) Michael Irvin, we knew we were going to be first-day players, we just didn't know where we were going to go," Blades said.

Going to facilities such as EXOS in California, Arizona, or Florida to train for the Draft back then wasn't as common.

For guys coming from Miami, their workouts leading up to the Draft were legendary because of everything stated above. The talent was there, but to be able to play with the confidence and swagger that "The U" played with, raised the competition as high as possible. Blades and his fellow Draft hopefuls would push each other so hard that Blades is convinced that pressure motivated them better than any trainer could have done.

Knowing he had the tape in college and the physical abilities that would translate to the NFL, Blades was confident he would be a high draft pick, but that doesn't mean his pre-Draft process came without any scares. Blades told the story, forgetting exactly which team it was.

"I got a real bad knock. I went for a physical there and they brought up an old injury I had since I was a little kid. I had a little chip on my third vertebrae on my neck. I said, 'Oh shoot, they sent that around to everyone' and the doubt starts going in your mind that my Draft status is going to fall, and I may not be as highly thought about. When I went out to (Los Angeles), which is when I originally fell in love with the Raiders because their owner, Al Davis, said 'Come on. We will fly you out. We'll do a medical exam.'"

In Blades' words, "Once the Bad Boys of the NFL" cleared him because it was just an old injury and they weren't worried about, he knew it ultimately wouldn't have a negative impact on his Draft stock. In the same way that failing one team's physical can spread around the league like wildfire, passing an Al Davis physical held even more stock in NFL circles.

With that behind him, Blades was able to continue to focus on working out and two weeks later, after one of his workouts, he had a conversation with the head coach of a team with one of the top picks in the 1988 Draft.

"The Detroit Lions' Wayne Fontes is in town looking at film. I'm thinking, okay, the Detroit Lions at that time needed everything: pass rushers, wide receivers, quarterback. They needed everything. I didn't think they needed me. We had just finished working out. I was going to my car and Wayne Fontes says, 'Bennie Blades.' I said, 'Yes, sir?' He said, 'I just finished watching film on you. I'll see you on Draft Day.' That was the extent of my conversation with Wayne Fontes, but every other team they brought you in, they talked to you, and did all of that other stuff. I'm thinking, the third pick is the Detroit Lions. There is no way I'm going to the Detroit Lions."

Not thinking that the Detroit Lions were going to select him, Blades had a feeling that there was one person who wouldn't let him pass. That was, of course, Al Davis of the Raiders. The Raiders certainly had the ammo to take Blades, owning three first round picks in 1988: #6, #9, & #25. "Only because Al Davis cleared me before all of the other teams in the National Football League, you know. I used to love the way the Raiders played when I was growing up with Jack Tatum and Lester Hayes. So, I knew, if nothing else, he wasn't going to let me fall past the Raiders," Blades said.

That's the beauty of the NFL Draft. What you think you know isn't always reality. For Blades, the Draft started out how he expected, at least for a few picks. "When Draft Day came, and Aundray Bruce went to the Atlanta Falcons and Neil Smith went to the Kansas City Chiefs, I'm thinking, 'Okay, just like I thought a bunch of linebackers and defensive ends.' Then I get a call sitting at home in my living room." Blades explained he didn't go to New York for the Draft because he didn't expect to go too high. "I'm sitting in my living room, the phone rings, they give me the phone. It's the Detroit Lions saying, 'We're going to pick you with the next pick.' If you go back and look at the footage, I thought it was a joke!" Blades laughed recalling how he couldn't believe a ten-minute conversation with Wayne Fontes led to him being selected third overall.

"Like I said, I had only met Wayne Fontes and so they call me back and they sent me a plane ticket. I go from Fort Lauderdale to Detroit Metro. I get off the plane, I take the stairs, and there's a helicopter waiting. They take me in the helicopter over to the Pontiac Silverdome because the Pistons were playing that night." The Pistons and the Lions shared the Pontiac Silverdome at that time. "Who introduces me at halftime? None other than Isiah Thomas. So, I'm like, whoa, I thought I was a rockstar in Miami. This is big time right here! My whole thing after that is I definitely cannot let this city down because you have the Pistons on a roll. They were the Bad Boys of the NBA and here is not only the man himself, Isiah Thomas, introducing me, but he does it at the Pontiac Silverdome in front of forty or fifty thousand people. So, I thought there is no way I can let this city down. It was a highlight of my career there."

While Draft Day certainly provided an element of surprise for Blades, sometimes surprises on Draft Day can make some players have a negative experience because they didn't go to the situation or location they wanted to go. For Blades, the shock not only didn't ruin his day, but the location was ironic.

"For me, it was all excitement because I tease with people all the time, I really wanted to be a Michigan Wolverine and I think they really would have gotten me," Blades said referring to being recruited by the University of Michigan out of high school. "But you took a kid from South Florida and during recruiting time you brought me up in the middle of January when it was cold as crap," Blades laughed. "I was like 'No, no, no, I'm not going to Michigan. It's cold up here!' and then to get drafted by Detroit and I was like 'Oh, I remember that'" Blades chuckled while reminiscing.

Blades would go on to have an outstanding ten-year NFL career, the majority spent as a member of the Detroit Lions, including a Pro Bowl berth in 1991. However, even for a player drafted third overall who spent a decade in the NFL, the Draft process still provides highs and lows. "The Draft is so funny because people think just because I am Bennie Blades, still the only Jim Thorpe Award winner down at the University of Miami, you can go from highs to lows at a drop of a hat. People can say, 'You're going top five and then you have a sucky Pro Day, and you go in the third round. That's the thing people fail to realize."

That is the Draft process in a nutshell, even for the guys who get picked right at the top like Bennie Blades.

CRIS CARTER
Before the Touchdowns

"I'M THE FIRST player to come to the NFL after three years of eligibility. It wasn't Herschel Walker, wasn't someone else. It was Cris Carter, and I'm the only Supplemental Draft player in the Hall of Fame, too."

Cris Carter is one of the greatest wide receivers the NFL has ever seen. If you grew up watching ESPN in the 1990s and early 2000s, you can still hear Chris Berman yelling 'All he does is catch touchdowns!' during Minnesota Vikings' highlights on *NFL Primetime*. However, Carter's football life didn't always seem destined for the endzone in the NFL or for a gold jacket in Canton, OH. This is the story about how one of the greatest players ever wound up being selected in the fourth round . . . of the 1987 Supplemental Draft.

Carter, an All-American wide receiver at Ohio State University, never played his senior season at Ohio State due to being ruled ineligible by the NCAA for accepting money from sports agent Norby Walters. The news of his ineligibility would come after the traditional 1987 NFL Draft had passed, so that left Carter having to enter the upcoming Supplemental Draft. However, especially at this time, the group of players entering the Supplemental Draft for this reason was not looked at so highly by NFL teams. Carter believes there may have also been some concerns with his speed as well that contributed to his falling to the fourth round, but he was never specifically told that was the case.

"On Draft Day, I was in my agent's office, and I talked to (Dallas Cowboys executive) Gil Brandt right before the Draft started. And he said Dallas was going to draft me in the first round. The phone call never came from Dallas, they didn't draft me. That's really the only experience that I had, and I got a phone call from (Philadelphia Eagles' head coach) Buddy Ryan saying I was on the Eagles, and they told me they had selected me in the fourth and then they started negotiating the contract. They were going to give me the salaries of the four first-round players because they really did believe I was a first-rounder, but my signing bonus was less than those guys and the season had already started. I was very, very satisfied that over the next four years I was going to make the same base salary as the guys that were drafted in the first round. So, I was excited— no training camp, no minicamps— just try and start Pro Football the next week after the Supplemental Draft."

Being drafted by the Eagles and Buddy Ryan was something the NCAA was also trying to discourage according to Carter. Why did it still happen then? "Because there was a discrepancy with NCAA, the NCAA declared that anyone who drafted me wouldn't be allowed on Ohio State's campus to recruit in the future. So, Buddy Ryan when he drafted me because we were talking, he was like, 'Man, they come up with this rule, I said f*** 'em! We're going to go to Ohio State any year and we're going to draft Carter now!' That's what he said. So that was my first experience, first conversation with Buddy Ryan," said Carter.

While Buddy Ryan still planned on being on Ohio State's campus in future years, Carter ended up back there not long after he even left due to the 1987 NFL strike. Talk about an unexpected, crazy way to get in and begin your NFL career.

Carter said there are very few one-percenters in the NFL who would have succeeded anywhere. "There's only a handful of them—Jim Brown, Randy Moss, Deion Sanders, Barry Sanders—there's only a handful of them. The rest of us need a system." That is what makes it even more incredible that Carter was able to find the success that he found in the NFL, because a lot of rookies would have crumbled under the same circumstances. Carter, though, never looked at his journey like that. "I haven't necessarily ever looked at it that way. The NFL is a grind, no matter when you come in. Even if you think you know the league, it's a grind, and there's all kind of traps that would allow you not to have a great career. There's all kind of excuses. It's just a matter of what do you make of them."

Carter has stayed involved in the NFL even after retirement, doing both television shows and podcasting. His personal experiences in that arena and the fact that he stayed actively in touch with today's NFL, would make Carter a great candidate to give out advice to college athletes with professional dreams. Carter's answer did not disappoint.

"I try to be consistent with this and I try to advise kids that they should stay in amateur football as long as possible and try to get their skill level as high as they can before they get playing against grown men for a living. Because football is a great game, but it's a different game just like anything else—cards, horseshoes—anything else when you put money on it. I don't think people understand the gravity of what grown men will do for a salary position to a dream job that they've been thinking about since they were kids. It's not a game anymore. It's a business. And how to understand the gravity around that as a young person is hard to impossible. I advise them to stay in school and play for free as long as you can. The typical example I give is a guy, twenty-eight or twenty-nine (years old), been playing in the league for five or six years. He might have a year or two left. He's got a wife, a couple kids, or if he isn't married, he's got a couple girlfriends, he's got a couple cars,' he's got a house, maybe a house he's trying to buy, maybe trying to build the house. And we don't calculate that when it's, 'Okay, what do I need to do to do this job? I got to take this job from a grown man who's maybe been getting paid by the NFL for five to seven years.' I'm going to tell you something, you walk up to the NFL pay window and you see the type of money for playing football. It changes you. It changes how you look at stuff, and to think that you can take that away from a man just because you went to Ohio State or Alabama or Florida, you got another thing coming. It isn't about that, it isn't about where you're from, man! It's about this thing that's called Pro Football and it's done a different way, and the only place they play it is in the NFL."

Carter's story is unique, to say the least. Carter led the NFL in receiving touchdowns in three different seasons, and finished his career with 130 receiving touchdowns, which is still good for fourth most all-time in NFL history. While not impossible, it seems the odds are unlikely that we will ever see another player elected to the Pro Football Hall of Fame who got his NFL start by being selected in the Supplemental Draft.

TERRELL DAVIS
Mile High Sleeper

ERRELL DAVIS IS regarded as one of the greatest running backs of all-time. To give you an idea about just how dominant Davis was, he made the Pro Football Hall of Fame while playing double-digit games in only four seasons in the National Football League. Only four times did Davis get a real chance to make an impact on a season. What he did in those four seasons was nothing short of remarkable, racking up 6,413 rushing yards, 61 total touchdowns, two Super Bowl championships, a Super Bowl MVP, a regular season MVP award, and earning three First Team All-Pro nods. As you can see, someone like Davis only needed four seasons to prove he belonged in Canton, immortalized in bronze until the end of time.

Those four seasons were right out of the gate for Davis who sprung onto the scene starting fourteen games as a rookie for the Denver Broncos. For someone to have that type of early success, you would assume he must have been a once-in-a-generation prospect who was drafted in the first round to be "'the man" from Day One, right? When it comes to Terrell Davis, that is the furthest notion from the truth.

The California kid stayed home for college attending Long Beach State, but after his first year there, the football program was cancelled. Davis was recruited by and attended the University of Georgia. When he arrived, he was on the bottom looking up a long, talented running back depth chart. Davis fought to get all the way to number two on the depth chart, but he was not going to surpass Garrison Hearst. Hearst went on to be an All-American and win the Doak Walker Award given to the best running back in college football in 1992.

With Hearst gone, Davis would have his chance to show the world what he could do in 1993 as the starting running back. What Davis didn't realize until later, though, was that he was very comfortable in the backup role. "When Garrison left my junior year, I went from being behind Garrison to becoming 'the man,' and I struggled with that. I didn't realize it until I became 'the man' that that role was tough. Like here at Georgia, the history there of the running backs—RBU—and I just struggled, man. I failed," said Davis.

Davis described his junior year as hit or miss, while the team struggled to win as well and finished just 5-6. Heading into his senior year, Davis was benched and moved to fullback in favor of another future NFL star: Hines Ward. Ward would turn into one of the NFL's best wide receivers of his generation, but while at Georgia he did it all, including playing running back in 1994.

When Davis was the starting running back, there was a time that he was rated the third best running back prospect for his Draft class. But once his season as the lead running back didn't go as planned, Davis admits he had no expectations to even get drafted. However, late in his senior year he felt the door was open again. "It was just a weird kind of season, but I finished the season off really good with two of my best games ever. So, when the Draft came around as much as you try to look at some of the articles, the pundits and the gurus (and) Mel Kipers and all—well, even Mel had me still rated as a third-round pick," Davis continued. "I was like, 'Okay, that's cool, that's cool, that's good.'"

Based on the information Davis could gather, he now felt comfortable and expected he would be taken in the third or fourth round of the 1995 NFL Draft. Well, the third and fourth rounds would come and go, and Davis was still available. For the late rounds, Davis was with his family and friends in

Atlanta and the moment was not as big as you would imagine. They actually found out when his name went across the bottom ticker on the television. Davis was taken by the Denver Broncos in the sixth round, 196th overall. It was bittersweet for Davis.

> "Number one, I never talked to Denver. I never saw Denver come out to my pro workouts, Pro Days, nothing. So, to hear Denver drafting me was kind of shocking because I had never spoken to them, and I thought the Cleveland Browns and the (Dallas) Cowboys were the two teams that showed the most interest to me. Which it wasn't a great deal of it, but I had spoken to them at Pro Days and spoken to them at the Combine, so I had thought the Cowboys for sure, if not the Cowboys, I was absolutely positive that the Browns would draft me."

On top of the surprise factor, another reason Davis wasn't excited about being taken by Denver was that the childhood San Diego Chargers' fan in him had disliked the Broncos most of his life! Fandom runs deep for all.

Davis recalls his agent confirming the selection, but as a sixth-round pick at the time, he never got the call from any

Broncos' coaches or brass personnel. As a matter of fact, to his knowledge, he doesn't remember ever speaking to head coach Mike Shanahan until he physically arrived in Denver. He spoke to a secretary and received a letter detailing key dates and travel itineraries, but that was it.

Davis was initilly realistic rather than optimistic since he was a late-round pick. He had seen it all too often where a former Georgia player would be drafted late and next thing you knew they were cut and back in Athens or Atlanta. Davis felt they didn't invest much in him to guarantee anything besides a few cuts and bruises as a "camp body." Davis' tune would change early on, however.

Once Davis got to the very first minicamp with the Broncos, he was able to size up his competition, and quickly noticed that he was in a great position. "No disrespect to anybody I saw, but my mentality was 'nobody on that roster is better than me' and that's what I thought. When I was flying back to Atlanta or going back to Athens, that was my mentality. I felt like I could beat out everybody we had on the roster."

Davis saw that the other guys all had their strengths like speed or size, but they always had a weakness, too. He believed he was the most complete running back there because he was the total package in terms of size, speed, blocking, catching, and running. He also knew that no one was going to outwork him from an energy or effort standpoint. Based on his quick start as a rookie in the NFL, it sure looks like Davis was spot on with his post-minicamp analysis.

It's always amazing to see a guy burst onto the NFL scene immediately, who struggled to find consistent success in college. It's not like Davis needed a ton of development and was years away from being a productive player. He walked out of college where he lost his spot to a future NFL wide receiver, and he became the best running back in football in less than twenty-four months. It's nothing short of remarkable, but it's what makes every Draft story unique. Players like Davis make scouts now dig even harder to find the diamonds in the rough, the guys that may be lost on a depth chart or lost in the shuffle in their college programs. Can you find the next Terrell Davis? I can tell you this much: if you do, your team will be better off.

BRETT FAVRE
Drafted ... Twice?

B RETT FAVRE'S CAREER is well documented as one of the greatest and most popular in NFL history. Favre won three Most Valuable Player (MVP) awards during his time in Green Bay as the Packers' quarterback. That also included two trips to the Super Bowl and winning Super Bowl XXXI. The end of Favre's career was always a talking point: mauling retirement, his year as a New York Jet, and ultimately finishing his career with a two-year stint with the Minnesota Vikings. In fact, the end of his career included one of his greatest seasons ever in 2009 when he finished fourth in the MVP and took the Vikings to the NFC Championship Game. Many will be surprised to learn, however, that the start to Favre's career almost didn't happen. He is the player who holds the record for most consecutive games started in a row in NFL history with 297, but what took place before that streak ever began is often forgotten.

Favre attended the University of Southern Mississippi (Southern Miss) where, much like his NFL career, it began in dramatic fashion. His freshman year, the team opened against a loaded Alabama Crimson Tide team that featured players such as future Pro Football Hall of Famer Derrick Thomas at Linebacker. "They were stacked and loaded. I didn't play and I'll be honest with you, I wasn't that upset that I didn't play," Favre joked. "The next week we played Tulane at home and Mack Brown, interestingly was the coach for Tulane. They had a really good team."

Before halftime, with Southern Miss down and looking for a spark on offense, Favre was inserted into the game at quarterback. He led them to a come-from-behind 31-24 victory. Favre started the next week against Texas A&M and never looked back.

"Going into my senior year, although I didn't redshirt, I had three years under my belt as a starter. That was a different time than it is now," Favre said. "If you threw for 1,500 to 2,000 yards, that would be kind of the equivalent of throwing for 4,000 or 4,500 in today's game. To give you an idea of how much we threw it, I threw 52 touchdowns in my career. Guys do that in the season (now), so you can't really base today's game in those years." Favre talked about how even back then, a few schools such as Houston and Florida had some prolific quarterbacks who put up huge numbers, but for Favre, it wasn't all about statistics.

"I can't have statistics that rival some of these other guys. I have the size and the thing that I knew, or felt like I knew, I could do better than anyone, not that it's something that's vitally important, but my arm strength and release were, I felt like, second to none. I wasn't going to break any forty-times (records), but I wasn't slow. I felt like I was slippery in the pocket, or I could use my legs to get me out of a lot of stuff, maybe not rush for a hundred yards, but buy a lot of time. I think people would agree with that throughout my career."

After his junior season, Favre knew there was no question that he could physically play in the National Football League. However, even a young Favre would have told you that he still needed experience understanding other concepts of the game.

"What I needed, and would have admitted I needed, was experience in regard to understanding blitzes, understanding the ins-and-outs of defenses, and fronts and coverages. Things I never really learned in college and no disrespect to my coaches, we were an option-team. We were a sprint-out passing team. I was a make-chicken-salad-out-of-chicken-s*** type of quarterback. They'd blitz everybody and rather than have a blitz call, I would just escape then make an unbelievable pass and we move on. I felt like from a schoolyard perspective, there was no one better."

All Favre needed was a great senior season with his natural abilities and he was first-round bound for the NFL Draft. However, on July 14, 1990, the summer before his senior season, Favre faced a giant challenge that could have cost him his life on.

"Going into my senior year I had the car wreck, and no one thought I would play. If I was trying to position myself for the first round and being the first quarterback taken, I probably would have been better off redshirting. I knew that. I really felt that way. I had thirty-six inches of my intestines removed August 8th. I had a fractured vertebrae in my lower back. I had multiple bruises, cuts, stitches, I mean, I was beat up really bad, but much like my career after college, I was determined to play to prove everyone wrong. Right or wrong. Should have, should not have. That was my mentality."

Favre miraculously went on to lead Southern Miss to victories over Alabama and Auburn his senior year and lost to Georgia by only one point. "Statistically speaking, in those games and throughout the year, it was modest at best, maybe subpar compared to previous years," Favre said, referring to battling through his final year in college.

Favre did just that, battle. But would impressive wins and gutsy plays be enough to overshadow those subpar individual numbers and prior health concerns? For future Green Bay Packers' general manager Ron Wolf, who at the time worked for the New York Jets, that final season didn't do Favre justice. Favre recalled, "(Ron) watched my senior year tapes and one of our coaches, a guy named Thamas Coleman said, 'Hey, what do you think?' and (Ron) said, 'Well, not bad.' (Coleman) goes, 'What did you watch?' and (Ron) said, 'I watched the senior year tapes.'"

Access to college film was not as easy to obtain as it is in today's NFL. Understanding that Ron didn't watch Favre's other seasons' games, Coach Coleman made sure Ron knew what a healthy Favre really looked like. "Thamas Coleman said, 'Hey, you know he had a car wreck?' (Coleman) basically told (Ron) you need to watch the other three years," said Favre. "Which Ron did, thankfully. He went back in and watched and walked out and said, 'I got to have this guy' and you know that's Ron's exact words, so I'm thankful for Coach Coleman and for Ron for a lot of reasons."

Favre's expectations for the Draft were high, but he understood that if other teams didn't put in the extra time like Ron Wolf had, that most teams would have some question marks about him. It wasn't only the senior-year tape that Favre knew scouts would have some concerns with either. It was all the other pre-Draft metrics such as the forty-yard dash and broad jump, which Favre wasn't off the charts at. Favre, knew there were more important attributes that he had in spades. "What's most important is can the guy play football? Is he a player? Is he a winner? Is he gritty? Is he tough? Is he a great leader? Those are the things that matter, and I felt like I did those very well, but I thought that I was going to be based off statistics, first and foremost, and I didn't know where that was going to position me in the Draft."

Attempting to grasp an idea of where he was going to land, Favre simply looked at who was showing the most interest in him by coming in to work him out. "Mike Holmgren came in and worked me out. I remember him telling me very clearly, he said, 'We're not drafting the quarterback early. We got Montana. We got Young,' he said, 'but I was sent here to work you out,'" Favre explained of Holmgren who was an assistant with the San Francisco 49ers at the time.

Favre recalled that the three teams that came in multiple times to work him out during the pre-Draft process were the Falcons, Raiders, and Seahawks. Unlike Holmgren and the 49ers, those three teams would be in the quarterback market early in the 1991 NFL Draft. Between them working him out often and Ron Wolf's extra film study for the Jets, Favre felt there was reason for optimism come Draft Day. "I was very hopeful, but as I sat there on Draft Day, I wasn't devastated with each pick that went by because deep down inside, I wasn't surprised. I really felt like I knew the Raiders and I knew the Seahawks were probably going to draft someone early and they both did in the first round. When those two picks were gone, I had a pretty good idea that I probably would go with Atlanta's third pick, which I did."

While Atlanta ended up drafting Favre with the 33rd pick, it almost left the window open for Favre's biggest fan. "Atlanta drafted two guys in the first round, not a quarterback, but I ultimately went to them. Had the Jets had a first-round pick, I would have gone with that pick. I was basically going to be their first pick, which was the 34th pick."

Ron Wolf may have been a pick away from landing Favre for the New York Jets in 1991, but that wasn't the end of the Favre-Wolf NFL Draft saga. Ron Wolf ended up becoming the Green Bay Packers' general manager prior to the 1992 NFL Draft. Instead of waiting until the Draft in April, Wolf made his first major move in February, sending Atlanta a first-round pick in exchange for Brett Favre. As valuable as first round picks are, especially for a first-time general manager, Favre to this day is still in awe of Wolf's guts to make that move.

"For a guy that no one heard of that (Atlanta) didn't play the first year, who had put on twenty-five pounds, not a good (twenty-five) pounds, did everything he could possibly do to get cut, and to get traded for a first-round pick when he was drafted in the second round. I mean, are you kidding me? I've told people this so many times and Ron obviously is in the Hall of Fame, deservingly so, but people, I think they under value or underestimate that decision that he made. He finally got a chance to be the GM for a team that had tremendous history, tradition, but had been idle for twenty-five years and was starving for a spark and he took a chance and really laid his whole career on the line and I have to be honest with you, I think he had more confidence (in me) than I had in myself, and I was pretty confident that I could turn a team around, but what twenty-two year-old in my position would say otherwise?"

It was certainly a gamble to say the least, but one only legends are made of. "He laid everything he had on one color, or one number, and it paid off," said Favre.

Paid off it did indeed, and for Favre, the second Draft pick that was used on him turned out to be the one that would catapult his legendary career. It is amazing how one man's trash can be another's treasure even in terms of NFL players. Favre went from an unwanted, second-rounder with some talent in Atlanta to a beloved, face-of-the-franchise star in Green Bay in less than a year. While every prospect hopes that they will be drafted to the perfect destination immediately, Brett Favre's story shows that sometimes being drafted twice isn't so bad after all.

BRAD JOHNSON
Almost Your Favorite Teacher

THE NFL CAN often be too big for even a great college player. The player may have dominated college football, but there are a few traits, such as speed and strength, that alone simply won't allow them to find high level success in the NFL against the absolute best players in the world. Legendary college players such as Tim Tebow, Eric Crouch, and Trent Richardson never found remotely the same success in the NFL during their college days. By no means should that diminish their college careers or who they were as football players, it's just the nature of the beast that is the NFL.

The opposite of that, however, would be a much shorter list. Less often, there is a player that didn't produce a lot in college or even play a lot, but turns around and has a long, successful NFL career. As rare as that is, enter Super Bowl champion quarterback Brad Johnson, who is one of the few that would qualify for this list.

"I started my junior year at Florida State, got benched in game six, I think. Then my senior year I started one game. I was behind my best friend, Casey Weldon, who was the runner-up to the Heisman and we were the number one team in the country and got beat—had a wide-right field goal. So, that's what people remember. I started one game because Casey got hurt," Johnson said.

Most people would assume that Johnson's NFL dreams would be shot at that point, but that was far from the case. In limited time, Johnson still managed to complete 64.7 percent of his passes in college and throw for fourteen touchdowns against nine interceptions. He also had the ideal size and athletic ability, the kind that allowed Johnson to play a few seasons on Florida State's basketball team as well. All of those factors intrigued the NFL enough for Johnson to wind up at the NFL Scouting Combine in 1992.

"I was fortunate enough to go to the NFL Combine. They only take seventeen quarterbacks that they actually invite, and then they invite three other quarterbacks to come up there a little bit earlier. We threw to the linebackers, the running backs, the (defensive backs)—all their drills—and then we actually went through the process, too, as 'the extra guys' and that was T.J. Rubley and Bucky Richardson. We threw, I tested in forty, and vertical and did all that kind of stuff. When I left, I thought I was the best quarterback, but every general manager and every coach did not have the same view I had."

The 1992 NFL Draft saw nineteen quarterbacks get selected over its twelve rounds. That said, there was plenty of quarterback talent. Leading up to the Draft, Johnson knew there was no guarantee he would ever play football again. "I was teaching middle school at Raa Middle School in Tallahassee, FL. I'd go there from 8:00am to 3:30pm every day and teach P.E. and then after that I'd go (train)." To be safe, Johnson spent January, February, and March finishing up his internship as 'Mr. Johnson.'

Johnson was convinced he was going to end up in one of two places because only two coaches came to work him out. First were the New York Giants. Then head coach Jim Fassel came and watched him throw and told him they were planning on taking a quarterback mid-round of the Draft. The second team was the Cincinnati Bengals and quarterback coach Dana Bible, who watched Johnson throw to his buddies wearing their jeans, nonetheless.

Johnson stayed in his dorm room with his dad for the Draft. Right away one of Johnson's two teams was wiped away as the Cincinnati Bengals selected quarterback David Klingler from Houston with the sixth pick in the first round. Now, Johnson was holding out all hope for Jim Fassel and the New York Giants, but that too was wiped away as they selected Kent Graham out of Ohio State in the eighth round. At that moment, all Johnson had was word that the Atlanta Falcons would bring him in as a free agent if he wasn't drafted, according to his friend who was an equipment manager there at the time. Johnson told his friend if he wasn't drafted, he was going to head back home to North Carolina and begin his career as a schoolteacher.

On the last day of the Draft, Johnson and his dad were watching the ticker on the screen go by. Johnson's dad liked to lay on the floor with a pillow behind his head and then suddenly he was no longer laying down.

"My dad kind of jumps up off the floor. He gets excited and I said, 'What happened?' He said, 'I think I saw your name and it came across the ticker.' I said, 'Well, who was it?' He said, 'I don't know. Let's wait,' and then it came back around again it said 'Minnesota Vikings, 227th pick.' I said, 'I guess we got drafted,' and then about three minutes later I get a call from Denny Green who was the head coach at that time. He just congratulated me. He congratulated me and all those kinds of things and said, 'Listen, pack your bags and we'll see you here in about four days.'"

So, how did Brad Johnson celebrate being drafted? No party, no clubs, no parade. He went to work out before taking two of his buddies and his dad out to eat.

While Johnson thought his best chance to get drafted was by a team who came and saw him workout right before the Draft, it turned out that event just actually happened years beforehand. At the time of the Draft, Jack Burns was starting his first year with the Vikings as their offensive coordinator and quarterback coach but Burns actually recruited Johnson out of high school while he was coaching at the University of Louisville. Burns knew Johnson's background and athletic makeup, so it made using a ninth-round flyer on him worth the risk.

When Johnson arrived in Minnesota, he came into a quarterback room with some familiar names: Rich Gannon, Sean Salisbury, and Wade Wilson. Right away, Johnson had a rookie moment that would turn into an ironic moment down the road.

"First day I sat in my chair in the team meeting room, Wade Wilson says, 'Get up, rookie' and I said, 'Okay.' That's been his chair for eleven years that he sat in, so I sat one chair back. Then they actually cut him that year for me, and he went on to play for the Atlanta Falcons and actually later became my QB coach in Dallas at the end of my career seventeen years later. That first year I didn't have a pair of turf shoes, so I wore Wade Wilson's turf shoes he left in his locker, and I took over his locker and wore those turf shoes that whole year, and then I sat in that seat that he used to sit in. That was my seat for the next seven years."

In other words, between the chair, the position, the locker, and the shoes, it's safe to say Johnson really did replace Wilson for the Vikings.

Johnson went on to finish his career with a record of 72-53 as a starting quarterback. He threw for 29,054 yards and 166 touchdowns in the regular season. What he is most remembered for, though, is winning Super Bowl XXXVII as the starting quarterback of the Tampa Bay Buccaneers. Johnson threw for 215 yards and a pair of touchdowns in the Buccaneers 48-21 win. That day, Johnson outdueled the Oakland

Raiders' starting quarterback, Rich Gannon, with whom he shared that first quarterback room in Minnesota back in 1992.

Johnson is a true testament that players peak at different points in their lives. Simply because a player doesn't find the field or a lot of success in college doesn't necessarily mean he won't have better days ahead. Sometimes all it takes is the right coach, team, or time and a player such as Brad Johnson can see it all come together. As in Johnson's case, that may even result in forever being a member of an elite fraternity: Super Bowl Winning Quarterbacks.

STEVE LARGENT
Not a Bum, Bum

W
HEN STEVE LARGENT retired from the NFL, he held every major career receiving record in NFL history: yards, receptions, and touchdowns. There was no denying he was bound for the Pro Football Hall of Fame as soon as he hung up his cleats following the 1989 season. It would be easy to assume that a player of his caliber was highly touted coming out of college. For Largent, however, that was not the case. As a matter of fact, his focus wasn't even entirely on the NFL.

"Let me tell you that the Draft was a very interesting thing when I came out of college," he began. "This was in 1976 and I felt that I could play at the next level but wasn't sure. I had really taken an effort to make sure that I graduated from college after my senior year. I didn't want to have to come back another year. I didn't want to have to stay in school, so

I graduated in May. I was a biology major, if you can believe that," Largent joked.

Largent knew he had a great college career being named a team captain, All-Missouri Valley Conference, and other accolades, but even with all of that, he wasn't sure what his future entailed. "The Draft wasn't something that I was concentrating on. I was concentrating on graduating. I obviously knew when the Draft was and that the Draft occurred in the morning through the afternoon, but I hadn't been watching what was happening," Largent said. "We had a Scout Day. They invited all the scouts that wanted to come to the University of Tulsa to come and take our forty-time and measure how tall we were and how much we weighed and all that kind of stuff. We did that and I did that."

Largent met up with some Tulsa teammates at the stadium and they were talking about when they all got drafted. He remembered being the fourth player from the University of Tulsa drafted that year. "I was drafted in the fourth round by the Houston Oilers, and I knew Bum Phillips was the coach down there. I had never seen a game that the Houston Oilers played. I didn't know a lot about Bum Phillips. I sure didn't know who the heck his receivers coach was," Largent said recalling he also only could name two wide receivers on the Oilers' roster at the time. "They contacted me after they drafted me, and said they'd be in touch with me and congratulations on being drafted in the fourth round."

While Largent may have been a fourth-round pick, he was actually the Houston Oilers' second draft pick in 1976. Houston drafted a tight end named Mike Barber out of Louisiana Tech in the second round and then used their next pick on Largent in the fourth round. Largent never expected to be taken by the Oilers because they never showed any interest in him before the Draft, but as he recalls, that was consistent with other teams as well. "In fact, no teams really had expressed a lot of interest in me. There were different people, the different scouts that came to our games and I didn't know who they were scouts for and I never talked to them. They never talked to me," said Largent.

That was Steve Largent's Draft experience. As he said, it just wasn't that big of a deal back then if you weren't a first-rounder and to him specifically it wasn't anything significant. The key to the Steve Largent story ended up being one of his assistant coaches while at Tulsa, Jerry Rhome. "I know Jerry Rhome was a real proponent of me and anybody and everybody he talked to, he touted me very high," said Largent.

Rhome left Tulsa after Largent's senior season to take an assistant coaching position with the Seattle Seahawks. According to Largent, Rhome was petitioning the Seahawks to draft

Largent, but that never happened. However, that connection would come in play down the line. "There was such a thing as recallable waivers so they would put you on the waiver wire and then reclaim you if anybody showed any interest and then try to work out a trade," Largent explained.

After a preseason game, Largent recalls the conversation he had with head coach Bum Phillips that would change the path of his NFL career. "Bum Phillips told me, 'Hey, we think you got a chance to play in this league, but it won't be for us. Good luck to you.' That was basically what he said."

At that point, Largent and his wife packed the few belongings they had into his Ford Pinto station wagon and a small U-Haul trailer. They left Houston to go back to Oklahoma City, not knowing what their next chapter was going to hold. "We were contemplating what we were going to do with our lives at that point," said Largent.

It didn't take long for the contemplation to stop. Largent's next move was a phone call away when the Seattle Seahawks traded a 1977 8th round pick for Largent.

> "The Seahawks called me and said, 'Hey Steve, we know you've been cut by the Oilers, and we'd like to give you another chance. If you'd like to try, there will be a plane ticket waiting for you in Oklahoma City and

come on up' and I said, 'Alright, I'll be there.' I knew Jerry (Rhome) was there, so that was encouraging to me, but what I didn't know was when I got to Seattle that he had employed all of the passing scheme that we had at the University of Tulsa, because he was the quarterback and receiver coach. So, he had taken our passing game from University of Tulsa and basically employed it for the Seahawks. I knew the nomenclature, I knew where to line up, how deep to run the routes, when the ball should be thrown, and all that kind of stuff because I've been doing it for three years at the University of Tulsa. So, that was a really big boost to me and my confidence when I came to Seattle."

Largent's talent and experience in that offense paid off right away as he caught 54 passes for 705 yards and four touchdowns as a rookie. He spent his entire fourteen-year Hall of Fame career in Seattle.

You can tell how far the Draft has come since 1976. If a team today traded their own second pick for a future seventh round pick (there aren't eight rounds today), the general manager and scouting department's jobs would be in jeopardy. How could they use their team's second pick on a player that they don't think can make their roster? It's baffling to look back on, but it's stories like Largent's that have put such an emphasis on the Draft for a few reasons. First off, use your highest draft picks on positions you believe can make your roster. Second, and most importantly, make sure you have done enough homework on a prospect so when you get a player of Largent's caliber in your doors, you don't give him away for fifty cents on the dollar.

TONY MANDARICH
Workout Winner &
A Bad Dinner

B Y THE TIME Tony Mandarich finished playing at
Michigan State University (MSU), he was not only
the most hyped-up offensive lineman entering the
NFL Draft, but arguably the most hyped-up offensive lineman
to ever enter the NFL Draft to that point in 1989. A lot of people know the story of Mandarich: Sports Illustrated covers,
steroids, and not reaching his enormous NFL expectations.
However, the story here is about the prospect, the potential,
and the man with whom NFL scouts fell in love. This is the
story of one of the greatest prospects to enter the NFL Draft,
who was taken in what turned out to be the greatest top five
in Draft history.

Mandarich always set goals that he could strive for, and they were all critical steps to becoming the player he wanted to be. His goals when he got to college were to become a starter, be named All-Big Ten, be named an All-American, win the Outland Trophy, and go on to be the first pick in the NFL Draft. Mandarich went on to achieve all but two of those. While he was named a finalist for the Outland Trophy in 1988, Auburn's Tracy Rocker would go home with the hardware. He still considered that accomplishing his goal because based on the fact that Tracy Rocker went in the third round of the NFL Draft a few months later. Mandarich felt "there might be some politics involved and that's nothing against Tracy and I don't have really a resentment about it." The other goal he did not accomplish was to be the first player taken in the 1989 NFL Draft. He didn't have to wait around much longer since he was the second player selected, but more on that in a bit.

There were two accomplishments Mandarich didn't originally set as goals for himself, but is proud of still to this day. One, which was a complete surprise to him, was finishing sixth in voting for the 1988 Heisman Trophy as an offensive lineman. He is also proud but holds a little resentment about the fact that his forty-yard dash times are not held in the same regard as other legendary times. "I don't know if it pissed me off as much as it just makes me laugh," Mandarich said. One reason why is because the records you will see at the NFL Scouting Combine are times that were run at the Combine only. Mandarich ran his times at MSU's Pro Day, so those aren't used as official numbers by the NFL. Nonetheless, Mandarich ran like nothing NFL scouts had seen before for his size.

"Around 4.64 was my fastest and at 308 (pounds) that day," explained Mandarich. He found it funny how many people would bring up the fact that he benched 225 pounds thirty-nine times because he knows people, even back then, were benching more reps than that. For Mandarich, the bench press was good, but the speed was his focus. "I was very proud of it, but they never talk about it. I know I ran it," said Mandarich who explained how he ran so fast that all the scouts thought they screwed up the time when they stopped their clocks as he passed the finish line. "Well, they all clicked it, and all went like this," Mandarich said pulling his hands close to his chest. "Put it to their chest. They all thought that they clicked it too early and screwed up, which I thought was hilarious because I didn't even notice it until Coach (George) Perlis told me and I turned around and then they started sharing it with each other. 'What'd you get? What'd you get? What'd you get?' That ended up being like a 4.68. That's what they kind of averaged it out to," said Mandarich.

Mandarich said his second forty caused the same reaction from the scouts, which would be even faster averaging out to be about a 4.64. "I was such a cocky S.O.B.," Manadrich laughed, "I turned around I said, 'If you want, I'll run 4.5' and they were like 'No, no, no, no no. We don't want you to pull a hammy.' I was such a d***," Mandarich chuckled.

Being touted to the magnitude Mandarich was would make many people believe their own hype, which Mandarich explained, can be good or bad.

"I believed that. I mean, my goal was to be the best. If I don't want to be the best at it, what's the purpose? There were times when I would train, and I remember running a conditioning drill, we run 220s, which was basically 200 meters, so we started on the curve of a track and finish on a straightaway. I would run sixteen of them. When I was in shape getting ready right before camp, I would run sixteen of them with a ninety-second break and my average time was probably like twenty-six (or) twenty-seven seconds. I remember the fastest I ever ran one was mid-twenty-four seconds. I just had a long stride, and I just had a gift to run. But the point of that story was one day, this was probably a month before camp, I was just gassed out. I was tired and I was like 'I'm going to skip the running today. I'll just do it tomorrow.' It's like 12:30 or 1:00 in the morning on a Wednesday going into Thursday morning, and this is probably July, I just can't sleep. It's just my conscience just won't let me sleep and all I can hear is the voice saying, 'You talk about wanting to be the best, but you don't want to do that work that the best do to be the best.' I got my a** out of bed, threw on my stuff, and ran those 220s at 2:00 in the morning."

In Mandarich's eyes, it was that belief in his own hype that drove his work ethic that morning. "I don't have to do it, but if I don't do it then I can't talk about being the best anymore."

Believing that you are the best was vital for Mandarich at that time and when Sports Illustrated came calling for the infamous cover, he let his self-belief lead the way. "When Sports Illustrated put that on the cover, they had asked me, 'Do you think you're the best?' and I'm sure I said, 'Well, yeah, that's my goal to be the best and it's my goal to be the best in the NFL, ever.' As the subtitle on the cover, they wrote (The Best Offensive Line Prospect Ever) and that was their opinion," Mandarich said.

While believing his own hype helped him never miss a workout before, seeing himself—shirtless—gracing the cover of *Sports Illustrated*'s 1989 NFL Preview touted in that way would negatively affect him down the road. "That was the downfall," Mandarich admitted. "You got to remember, the media outlets, there was no internet. *Sports Illustrated* was like the 800-pound sports gorilla. That's when I was like 'Wow, man. These guys put me on the cover and they're saying this? Holy smokes.' That was a big downfall when I started to believe that press, like something shifted in me, you know? As soon as I started to believe it, the first step off the cliff happened."

The first five picks of the 1989 NFL Draft landed four players in the Pro Football Hall of Fame when their careers were over.

The top five picks were as follows:

1. Dallas Cowboys—Troy Aikman, UCLA, QB

2. Green Bay Packers—Tony Mandarich, Michigan St., T

3. Detroit Lions—Barry Sanders, Oklahoma St., RB

4. Kansas City Chiefs—Derrick Thomas, Alabama, LB

5. Atlanta Falcons—Deion Sanders, Florida St., DB

It's very easy to see how each of their careers turned out now in hindsight, but at the time, Mandarich was not seen as a reach by any stretch of the imagination. Again, this is the greatest offensive lineman prospect of all-time. The Packers were just thrilled he was going to be there for the second pick, and they told him so about a week prior. "I knew a week before," Mandarich explained. "They told me because Dallas came out publicly to the media and said, 'We are going to take Troy,' because I'm sure that they worked him out at the Combine and I'm sure they had their personal workout with him, and they were like 'We're taking Aikman.' Green Bay, I think came out to the media and said, 'If they hold up their word and they take Aikman, we're going to take Tony.'"

One team, the Cowboys, made it clear they would not be selecting him. Mandarich made it clear to another team in the top five that they better not take him, either.

"I'll tell you there was a story, crazy, it's a crazy story. I mean, it's embarrassing when I think about it, but it's funny as s***. Schottenheimer and Peterson [Kansas City Chiefs head coach and general manager] want to take me out to dinner. Pretty much to kind of get to know me. So, we sit down at this nice place. I remember the name of it, it was called 'Pistachios,' it was a nice seafood-steakhouse in East Lansing, (MI). We're sitting down at dinner and it's literally me and them two. I don't think there's anybody else. Maybe they had brought in like an assistant or scout or something? I don't know, but we're sitting there talking everything professional. I mean, I dressed up, put a jacket and tie on and I met them there and we sat down and we ordered appetizers and then we ordered dinner and then before dinner came, they were asking me 'So, we have some questions.' And I'm like, 'Absolutely, ask whatever you want.' So, Marty's first question was 'Have you ever done steroids?' I was like 'No, I've never tested positive for steroids.' Which is no lie at that time. They're like, 'Yeah, we know you never tested positive, but have you ever done them?' I was like 'No.' Because I thought, you admit yes to this it's going to cost you a lot of money probably and where you're drafted, all this stuff. So, I said 'No.' Then he kind of surprised me because he's like 'Well, we don't believe you' and I said, 'Well, what do you want me to do? I mean, I'll drug test for you right now if you want, or tomorrow, or whenever' because I was already off the stuff for six months because I knew Combine was coming up and I wasn't taking it during the season and all that stuff. I stopped like early season. I said, 'I'll do a drug test now if you want.' And they're like 'No, we just don't believe that you never took steroids this whole time,' and I said, 'What makes you believe that?' and they're like, 'Well, people just don't run as fast as you did and they don't play against defensive lineman like you do, like it's just an uncommon thing.'"

Mandarich went on to tell them that was just how he played. He played every play as if it was his last, which was an answer that wouldn't sway Schottenheimer's opinion on the matter stating again that he did not believe him. "I got irritated," said Mandarich who then told them, 'You don't have to believe me. F*** you. You have the fourth pick. I won't even f****** last past the second pick so you'll never have a fighting chance to draft me and if I do last to the fourth pick, don't f****** take me because I'm not going to play for Kansas City.' I got up and just nicely walked out. Never had dinner."

Mandarich did not have to worry about Kansas City selecting him because Green Bay did, in fact, take him with the second pick. He spent three seasons there. After a four-year hiatus from the NFL, Mandarich returned as a member of the Indianapolis Colts. During his time in Indianapolis, he became good friends with Colts' owner, Jim Irsay. Years later,

Irsay invited him to attend the Colts' game at Kansas City with him in the visiting owner's suite. Ironically that day, Marty Schottenheimer was also a guest in Kansas City's owner's suite for the game. Mandarich was hoping to run into Schotten-heimer and he got his wish, but what Mandarich said to him is not what you would expect. "I said, 'I just want to apologize for acting like such a j****** back in 1989 at that dinner' and he looks at me, again, just shocked as s***," Mandarich laughed. Mandarich admits that some of his antics when he was younger were not his best moments, but he believes own-ing them is important. "It's taking accountability and then not acting that way anymore."

WARREN MOON
The Draft's Total Lunar Eclipse

E VERYONE KNOWS ABOUT quarterback Warren
Moon's illustrious NFL career: seventeen seasons,
nine Pro Bowl selections, and 291 career passing
touchdowns. All of which helped Moon become the first
African American quarterback selected to the Pro Football
Hall of Fame. However, for Moon, getting the opportunity
to begin that seventeen-year career would be the most chal-
lenging part.

Moon's ideal size, arm talent, and label as the 1977 Pac-8
Player of the Year should have given the perfect momentum
leading into the 1978 NFL Draft. Yet, the future Pro Football
Hall of Fame quarterback spent his first six professional football seasons in . . . Canada? How is that possible?

"It was a totally different time compared to what they
do with the Draft now," Moon said in terms of how the NFL

scouts and evaluates a player. "We used to just have a senior workout, a senior day before the season started. They would come out and send us through the forty-yard dash and measure you and all those different things. Then they kind of used that information for that particular season. We did do the Wonderlic test and all that."

Without having the traditional NFL Combine at the time, Moon had to rely on that workout prior to his final year at the University of Washington to give NFL teams those metrics.

"They had scouts come out again and look at you one more time after the season was over, but that was pretty much it. There weren't any individual workouts or there weren't any teams that came out just to watch you throw the football or see if you could do the things that everybody was saying that you might be deficient at. That part of it was totally different at this time. I had hired an attorney at that time, Leigh Steinberg, and he was pretty well known, and he had already represented the first overall pick in the Draft in '75 in Steve Bartkowski, so he was pretty well versed on what the whole process was about at that time. He started doing all the due diligence on me with the other teams around the league, just seeing what the scuttlebutt was, because that was the only way you could really find out."

In 1978, Mel Kiper Jr. was still many years away from appearing on ESPN as the Draft guru. There wasn't even close to the media attention, both print and television, that the Draft generates today. "(Leigh Steinberg) just will call teams straight out, even called the general managers or personnel directors, and he started to get information on what people thought about me. And a lot of the information that he got back was that I either was going to get switched positions to a defensive back or wide receiver, (or) I might get drafted somewhere between the 10th and the 12th round of the Draft if I got drafted at all as a quarterback," Moon said, mentioning that the NFL Draft had twelve rounds in 1978.

"I gathered all that information to go along with what I was hearing from the Canadian Football League (CFL), which would come down to meet with me. And we sat in a film room at the University of Washington, me and their head coach Hugh Campbell, and we watched tape together. (We) watched tape of my games. We watched tape of CFL games to give me kind of a feel of what the CFL game was about. He told me not only did he think I could be a great quarterback in the Canadian Football League, but he also thought I could be a great quarterback in the National Football League. He told me that at that time and he wasn't aware what the interest was on me by the NFL, but that was his feeling."

When Moon went back to talk with Steinberg, who had already spoke with the Edmonton Eskimos, they compared the two options. Moon laughed as he elaborated on the decision.

"It was basically going to be like a high second round draft pick in the NFL. That's the kind of money that they were offering. I kind of went with the pros and the cons of everything that I had heard over that time, and I decided I was going to go play in Canada because they were going to give me a chance to play quarterback first of all, and that's something that I was diligent on doing. I didn't feel like I could play another position as a pro. I had never played another position since I was eleven-years old. I had been very, very good at the quarterback position at every level that I had played, so I just felt like I deserved an opportunity to play, or at least get a chance to play quarterback.

That's what my mindset was. I made the statement even way back then that if they had a league in Siberia and they were going to let me play quarterback, that's probably where I would have went."

Moon's decision came with some urgency. "There was a little pressure put on me because I did have to sign earlier because their season starts a lot earlier than the NFL season and their training camps started earlier, so I had to give them a decision," Moon explained that had he decided not to sign with the Eskimos, and instead ultimately decided to sign with the CFL.

"I've forsaken my opportunity to go through the NFL Draft even though I still could have been drafted by NFL teams, nobody decided to draft me and keep my rights, which is something I'm glad that didn't happen because that's what allowed me to be a free agent when I did come back to play in the NFL. Otherwise, some team would have had my rights if I would have gotten drafted that day and I'm surprised that nobody would even just take a flier as a twelfth-rounder and drafted me, but no one did, and that just kind of showed what they thought of me at that time."

While those are the details of Moon's decision to go to the CFL out of college, it still leaves questions about why he was in the situation to have to make that decision in the first place. Here is a player that checks every box yet found himself seemingly undesirable to NFL teams as a quarterback prospect. Where was the disconnect? What were the conversations and feedback Moon received?

"Most teams thought I was too small, or I wasn't tall enough. I'm the same height now that I was when I came out of college. I wasn't 220 (pounds) when I came out of college—only about 205 to 208—but I ended up playing in Canada my first year at 215. So, it had nothing to do with my size," Moon said, putting one critique to bed. "People said my arm wasn't strong enough. That was the best characteristic I had in my in my arsenal, how strong my arm was. They said I didn't come out of a prostyle offense, which I didn't, but a lot of college quarterbacks don't come out of a prostyle offense and that doesn't mean they don't get drafted. The excuses that I was hearing just didn't coincide with what the facts were," Moon explained.

The feedback Moon heard seemed odd and not only because of the career Moon eventually had in the NFL, either. Even as a prospect coming out of college, it's apparent that the reasons above clearly seemed contradictory to the player he was. Moon explained that he knew there was more to it.

"I knew it had more to do with than just my ability, I just I knew it did. It had to do with the color of my skin and a lot of different instances and even Doug Williams who went in the first round that year out of (Grambling State University). If John McKay wouldn't have drafted him, who used to have African American quarterbacks at (University of Southern California) all the time. He had Jimmy Jones and a bunch of other guys as quarterbacks. He wouldn't have probably went from (seventeenth) overall to Tampa. I knew it had something to do with that as well and that's something that I couldn't fight against. I knew it was going to be difficult for me to play the position of quarterback when I first decided to play it when I was eleven years old because I just knew there weren't a lot of people playing the position that looked like me. And I knew it was going to be an uphill battle, and I knew kind of the history of the position with other guys who had played in the NFL before me. There was a mentality back then about quarterbacks that were really good athletes that they would rather put them in another position than make them a quarterback because, at that time when I came out, quarterbacks weren't great athletes. They were 6-foot-4, 220 pounds, and they kind of stood in the pocket and threw the football, but they weren't guys that were going to do much else. I think that's kind of what most teams were looking for back in those days and I got looped into that. I got looped into that crowd of guys that were more athletic than anything else. I remember one time when I ran the forty before my senior year I kind of slowed up at the tapes. I didn't want to run too fast because I didn't want teams to think I was faster than what I was, and (then) they would want to move me. Because I had heard the stories about 'Oh, this guy runs a 4.5; he should be somewhere else' or 'this guy runs 4.4; we can put him on the corner, he'd be a better athlete at the corner position' so I would ease up on purpose just to not run as fast. I ran like a 4.65 just to make sure that I wasn't running too fast to be a quarterback."

Moon's athleticism turned out to somehow be a negative for him in his eyes in 1978. Thankfully, the NFL seems to have come around and revere athleticism at the quarterback position today with some of the greatest athletes in the world playing quarterback, and Moon knows it. "Oh yeah, it's totally different now. No question about it. These guys are all getting opportunities and they can show what they can do, and I don't have any problem with it today, but it did exist back then," Moon expressed.

Moon spent six of the best years of his football career in the CFL due to false narratives in 1978, and then saw those same narratives become accepted as positive qualities in today's game. It wouldn't be hard to see how Moon might have envy or regret regarding his missed opportunity. Moon, however, reacted pleasantly the opposite.

> "The thing that I don't regret is that I did go to a good organization that really wanted me. I went to a team that we won five championships in a row, which has never been done in any sport in professional sports since then. No team has won five championships in a row, so that's something I can always feel special about that time in my life. I got a chance to really play a lot of good football when I was up (in Canada). There's no other player that's ever been inducted in the Pro Football Hall of Fame and in the Canadian Football of Fame. I'm the only player that has that, so there are some positives to me going up there to

play that I can always look back and say, 'It wasn't the worst decision in the world.'"

While Moon's NFL career may have had the statistics, the longevity, and the accomplishments as if he was drafted right out of college, one wonders what could have been if he was scouted and evaluated correctly. Imagine taking Warren Moon's career accomplishments already listed above and adding six seasons of NFL football to them. Remember, Moon was polished coming right out of college. He wasn't a guy who needed to sit for a few seasons to work on mechanics. He began his professional career by winning the Grey Cup in five of six CFL seasons. Moon would have been a superstar very early on in the NFL, too.

Moon, like many before him and many after him, are true trailblazers for not just athletic quarterbacks, but African American quarterbacks as well. To think that the color of his skin could have created any negative narratives about his ability to play quarterback is heartbreaking. But it was guys like Moon, who had the perseverance and determination to go through the process the hard way and still achieve their dreams, that changed the narrative. Moon's Draft story is one of many that have positively influenced the way quarterbacks are allowed to play, the way scouts evaluate, and how dreams become realistic.

AARON RODGERS
Not What You Think

"**W**ITH THE FIRST selection in the 2005 NFL Draft, the San Francisco 49ers select..." Everyone knew leading up to the 2005 NFL Draft that those were going to be fourteen words announced from, then commissioner, Paul Tagliabue's mouth. The only question was would the last two words of that sentence be: "Alex Smith" or "Aaron Rodgers?"

Smith was the dual-threat signal-caller for head coach Urban Meyer and the Utah Utes, who were coming off an undefeated season. Rodgers, a California native, finished up his second season with the University of California (Cal), leading them to a 10-2 record after a previous stint at Butte Junior College.

However, before we dive into how the first pick shook out in 2005, let's take it back to the beginning of 2004 to find out when Rodgers found out he was even being touted as a guy of this caliber.

"I read an article in a magazine, I want to say it was *Sports Illustrated*. It's probably the beginning of 2004 and there was an article written because, at the time, both Mike Williams receiver for the USC Trojans, and I believe Maurice Clarett (from Ohio State) were both not really going to school; (they) were trying to enter the Draft as sophomores," Rodgers explained.

The rule stated that a player couldn't enter the NFL Draft until they were three years out of high school, so neither Williams nor Clarett were technically eligible for the Draft, but they were fighting for the rule change. The article listed players who, if there was no age requirement, could be drafted in the first round in 2004. The article listed Mike Williams . . . Maurice Clarett . . . and Aaron Rodgers.

"I remember thinking, man, we played 14 games (and) I started 10 games that season. I had a nice little season. I had a nice bowl game—threw for 400 (yards), rushed for couple touchdowns, but I didn't realize that people knew who I was on a national level. When I read this article, I was thinking, 'Man, okay, I guess my name is out there and people do know that I have talent, but first round?' I'd never thought about myself as a first-round player until I read that article."

Rodgers believed in himself and knew that he was going to become a good player. What he didn't know was that the country not only was taking notice, but they also already knew he was at that level.

Fast forward back to 2005 and Rodgers had declared for the NFL Draft, forgoing his senior season at Cal. The California kid was available and his favorite team as a child held the first overall pick—match made in Heaven, right? Rodgers recalled heading out to meet with the San Francisco 49ers brass, which first included a lunch at a haunted hotel with head coach Mike Nolan and offensive coordinator Mike McCarthy. After the lunch they headed up to the 49ers' facility where the grill session would begin. "I remember distinctly I was in a room with all their personnel people, and I was in the middle, and they were all around me and just popping, firing questions at me. 'What about this? What about this situation? How would you handle this? Who's most important in your life?'" Rodgers continued, "I remember doing that. I feel okay about it, but I didn't have this amazing, 'I'm definitely going number one to San Fran,' feeling even though I asked Mike McCarthy and he said that he thought that they were going to take me."

Rodgers recalled meeting with the Miami Dolphins and their head coach at the time, Nick Saban, in person. He also visited the Cleveland Browns, but did not walk away from either of those meetings blown away with the impression he was going to end up at either spot. Then came the team that Aaron Rodgers felt he could end up with, and it wasn't the San Francisco 49ers like most people believe it to be.

"Tampa worked me out. They were at the number five pick, and Jon Gruden was the head coach and Paul Hackett was the offensive coordinator, and I had known who Paul was because I was a big Niner fan growing up and (Paul) always worked with Bill Walsh and they were big West Coast (offense) founders. So, I'd known exactly who Paul was and I remember meeting in the QB room again. It was like (then Cal head coach) Jeff Tedford and myself and Paul and Jon, and they had me on the board, talking ball, and we're watching some film. And (Jon) goes, 'Hey, would you be willing to work out?' and I'd already talked to Chase Lyman, one of my (Cal) receivers, and Garrett Cross, tight end for (Cal), and one of our backs, and said, 'Hey, there's a good chance I'm going to work out today so if you guys are around that would be awesome.' They're all juiced because they were all seniors trying to get drafted themselves."

Already prepared for the question from Gruden, Rodgers agreed to work out for the Tampa Bay Buccaneers that day. Rodgers wasn't the only one prepared for the workout, though. Gruden, not knowing if Rodgers would have any receivers around to throw to at the last minute, had one of his old players already at Memorial Stadium ready to run routes for the quarterback. As Rodgers, his Cal teammates, and the Bucs' brass are on the field, none other than arguably the greatest wide receiver in NFL history, Jerry Rice, comes walking on the field. "I was a huge Niner fan. Jerry (Rice) and Joe (Montana) were my favorite players, and so that was an absolute thrill. I was as nervous as you could possibly imagine every time that he was up. It was like, Chase was up, and I'd throw a perfect one. Garrett Cross, tight end, was up I'd throw him a great one. Jerry would be up in the line, and I'd just get so nervous," Rodgers laughed. "I was having a hard time throwing him the ball just because I was trying to be perfect."

Rodgers felt good after and as the Draft approached, he believed he was going to end up in the top eight. Of course, Tampa Bay was sitting at five and Rodgers received a call a few days before the Saturday Draft that seemed to be a great sign of things to come. "Jon Gruden called me on that Thursday, and I was already in New York, and he said, 'Hey, I just want you to know we love you. If you're at five, we're definitely taking you. If you fall to five, we're definitely taking you,' and I said, 'Awesome.'"

Rodgers was happy to possibly head to Tampa Bay. He really enjoyed meeting with Gruden and the Bucs' staff, and he also knew with their current quarterback situation that he would have an opportunity to start early on in the season. The only question now was whether he would be available at number five and, if not, would it be San Francisco who swipes him up? Surprisingly, Rodgers never felt that was a huge possibility.

"I didn't really have conversations with Mike Nolan. To be honest, the meeting that we had I didn't come away from it going, 'Man, I'd love to play for this guy. This is exactly the kind of guy I want to play for,' It didn't feel like that at all. I enjoyed Mike (McCarthy). I thought that Mike was very knowledgeable. He was a West Coast guy like me, meaning the West Coast philosophy. I love the West Coast philosophy because I grew up watching San Fran, so I enjoyed Mike. I enjoyed his stories, and thought it'd be fun to play for him as the offensive coordinator, but I didn't get a great vibe from Mike Nolan, and honestly, as we were told later, he didn't get a great vibe from me. He said that the things that were most impressive about Alex were that 'He pulled out his chair for his mom and I looked in his eyes and saw the guy that I wanted,' which is fine. It's totally fine. I love Alex. Alex is an amazing, amazing guy and it's obviously worked out well for me, and Alex had a nice, long career himself."

By the time the Draft rolled around, Rodgers really believed he had a great chance of falling to Tampa Bay because he knew all signs pointed towards San Francisco taking Alex Smith. Even though they never told him directly that they weren't taking him, Rodgers knew it was close to a done deal. While he also met with the Miami Dolphins who held the second pick, Rodgers knew they were likely going to take a running back. Rodgers and his team believed five was a great spot. If something happened, though, they viewed number eight and the Arizona Cardinals being the lowest he would fall since his meeting with Arizona and their head coach Denny Green at the NFL Scouting Combine went fantastic.

As many of you know by now, Tampa Bay and Arizona both went in different directions leaving Rodgers still available for the pick after number eight. However, even with everything already mentioned, this was not a huge surprise to Rodgers due to one misconception about the NFL Draft.

> "I think because there's so many leaks, there's probably not as many surprises for the players. They try and make it more dramatic on TV when you're watching it like, 'I can't believe this. This guy probably thought for sure he was going there.' There's not that many surprises. I mean, you kind of know. We sat down three hours before I was supposed to head to the Javits Center and my agent said, 'Look, unless something happens between fourteen and sixteen, which is like Carolina, (Kansas City, and Houston), it's going to be a long night probably because it looks like these other teams are out of it.' So, there's not that many surprises."

Rodgers' agent was correct and he fell all the way down to number twenty-four, where he was selected by the Green Bay Packers. Some of the most famous footage on Draft Day includes Rodgers waiting in the Green Room to be picked and ESPN's Suzy Kolber interviewing him to see if he knew what happened and why he might have fallen. Rodgers had a good understanding of the situation and mentioned that he knew the magnitude of pressure it puts on a franchise to draft a quarterback in the first round. These things happen, and because of the communication with his agent prior to the Draft, he wasn't all that surprised.

Rodgers acknowledged that they do a better job now with the Draft having less time between picks. However, he would advise prospects not to attend the Draft if they are invited based on his experience, which is not solely for the reasons you would imagine.

> "Craziest part about it was they were cleaning up the room around me. Yeah, they had a camera on me, but they didn't have the angles—the other angles. I was the last one in the Green Room. They were cleaning up this thing. They had a camera on me the entire time, which is kind of strange, so at one point it was just like, 'Alright, why don't you go hang out in the hallway and just take like thirty minutes because nothing is going to happen until the twenty-second pick,' and I was like, 'Alright.' That was a little bit strange, for sure."

Rodgers' fall to twenty-four didn't just mean a lower payday and move forward. This also meant he was heading to a place where he knew immediately that there would be no chance to see the field for a while. The Packers already had a legendary, future Hall of Famer at quarterback in Brett Favre. Due to the success Rodgers has had in his career after sitting behind Favre for three seasons, he is now the poster boy for all the "why quarterbacks shouldn't start right away" conversations that happen every single year around Draft time. The real question though is did Rodgers think he needed to sit that time for his development, or is just something the media assumes is ideal?

"I think that after having years to contemplate that, I don't think I needed to sit. But I think it was by far the best thing that could happen to me because I needed a reset of my own ego without having to go through the growing pains of being a starter and getting beat up, and it was best for me the way that it went down because I think it wouldn't have happened maybe as quickly for me if I've been playing. Or maybe it would have been a harder fall if I've been playing. For me, it was perfect because I literally showed up to Green Bay and I had a guy right in front of me who was significantly better than me, and it was the first time in my life that I saw somebody who was significantly better than me in the same quarterback room and it allowed me to go, 'Okay, wow. I have a long way to go. So, what am I going to do?' and I just set my mind to studying the heck out of Favre and seeing how he went about his business. And the things that he did that I couldn't even come close to doing, I watched very, very intently and figured out how to do them. And the things that I wanted to do differently, sock those things away in my mind or write them down, but if I ever get a chance, I want to do this this way. But all these things that I can't do yet, but he does without even thinking of it, I got to figure out how to do that. Otherwise, I'm never going to become the quarterback that I want to become. So, for me it was absolutely about the best thing to happen."

Rodgers mentioned how a lot of the quarterbacks these days who are drafted in the first round don't have the opportunity to be in the same room as a guy who is better than them. They don't have the player who can help show them what greatness is, whether directly or indirectly. For Rodgers, that time with Favre was invaluable. "When you get to watch what greatness looks like every single day, you have no other option, but to soak up as much as possible and that was a gift that falling twenty-four spots gave me."

It is truly a gift that benefitted both Rodgers and the Green Bay Packers tremendously. The story, however, is about the teams that now view Rodgers as the "The One That Got Away," and no team more than the Tampa Bay Buccaneers, not even the San Francisco 49ers. The 49ers had an instant connection with another quarterback early on, who had a successful career for them. The Bucs' head coach thought he was landing a franchise changing quarterback just days before the Draft, but instead the University of Auburn's second best running back prospect that year would be selected by Tampa Bay. Gruden's next and final four seasons in Tampa Bay would be quarterbacked by Chris Simms, Brian Griese, Bruce Gradkowski, Tim Rattay, Jeff Garcia, and Luke McCown. With all due respect to those players, they weren't quite Aaron Rodgers, one of the greatest players to ever touch a pigskin.

MIKE SINGLETARY
Knowing Your Worth

"I was pissed off. I was ticked at everything I was hearing leading to the Draft. Matter of fact, there was one scout that came to the stadium, this was the spring going into my senior year. I was walking, I was going to the training room, and he said, 'Excuse me, can you tell me where I can find Mike Singletary?' and I said, 'That's me' and he said, 'Oh no, no, no no, I mean seriously, where is Mike Singletary?' I said, 'I am him.' He said, 'No, I just finished watching film and I don't think you're that guy.'"

That was the beginning of what would be a common theme for Singletary during the scouting and pre-Draft process. Singletary would have to walk the scout to the trainer room where someone could vouch for him that he really was Mike

Singletary. The scout was surprised to say the least because he couldn't believe the player that he saw on film was as small as Singletary was in person. It's safe to say Singletary was not pleased with the conversation after the scout explained to him that he just didn't meet the required measurements for line-backers on their team. That's right—the intense, elite Monster of the Midway who gave opponents fits as one of the most terrifying linebackers the NFL has ever seen—wasn't looked at as an ideal linebacker to scouts back in college.

Singletary still couldn't imagine a situation where he wouldn't end up being selected in the first round of the 1981 NFL Draft. He was coming off back-to-back All-American seasons at Baylor University where his tackle numbers are that of legendary stature. Surely his dominance on film, tenacity, and football IQ would outweigh being slightly undersized, right? Unfortunately for Singletary, like many other prospects before him and after him, not being the ideal size apparently was a consistent knock against him around the league.

Even with that being his consistent feedback, Singletary still was hopeful he was going to be selected in the first round. He recalled getting calls from three separate teams, all of which said it was between him and another guy, and all three went with the other guy.

"At the end of the first round, I went outside. I had to leave. I just got up and went outside. I was very frustrated. I was crying, I was pissed, kicking tires, and I said, 'I'm not even going to play in the NFL. These guys have no idea what they're doing.' After all the complaining and whining and everything else I just stopped, I said, 'Lord, if you want me to play in the NFL, show me a sign. Let me get drafted in the second round by the Chicago Bears.' About five seconds later, my girlfriend, who's my wife now, came outside and said, 'Mike, the Bears just drafted you in the second round.' Wow. My mom was there, my girlfriend was there, and I was happy that I got picked, but I was very frustrated."

Singletary had a tremendous chip on his shoulder heading into his rookie season, but first he had to work out his contract. It turned out to be a tough negotiation because Singletary was set on being paid like the first-rounder that he believed he was. Singletary hired a Baylor friend named Jim Bob Byrd who was in law school to help him negotiate his contract. Byrd did not have any experience in these negotiations, yet Singletary assured him that he could do it, even after the first meeting ended with Byrd calling Singletary crying because of how the

Bears' front office executive Jim Finks spoke to him. Singletary motivated him to get back in there and have confidence in himself. "I end up getting a contract from the Bears and the first contract they offered me was like $25,000, which was notorious for the Bears to do and kind of lowball you to begin with. They sent me a $25,000 contract and I got the contract like, 'What the crap is this?' Everybody said, 'Hey man, that's what the GM's do is send you a lowball contract, just ignore it, it doesn't make sense.'"

At that point, the only real leverage Singletary thought he had was to hold out, which is exactly what he did. Singletary remained in Houston and continue to work out to stay in pristine shape. During one of his workouts, a very suave gentleman got out of his car, jacket over his shoulder, sunglasses on, and watch Singletary work out. That gentleman was Jim Finks of the Chicago Bears. Finks and Singletary talked and ultimately Finks convinced Singletary not to mess up his career before it even started. The Bears viewed him as a special player and if he believed he was a first-round caliber player, then he needed to prove it on the field and then negotiate his second contract using that proof. Singletary left the conversation and knew he better get to camp, which he did on the last day, which just so happened to be a live scrimmage. Singletary played so well in that scrimmage that the Bears cut their starting middle linebacker Tom Hicks, because they recognized there was a new Monster of the Midway in town.

Singletary spent his entire twelve-year Pro Football Hall of Fame career with the Bears. He earned ten trips to the Pro Bowl, won two Defensive Player of the Year awards, and led the 1985 Bears, and arguably the greatest defense of all-time, to a Super Bowl victory. Singletary experienced something many prospects go through during the Draft process. Their measurables may be viewed negatively, even if their college film shows it does not matter because height is one of the few traits you can't work to improve. It can be frustrating and ultimately create a very negative experience for prospects during this time. However, if Singletary's story shows anything, it's that if you get an opportunity, you can still prove all the doubters wrong and work to earn the contract you knew you deserved from the beginning. Singletary always knew his worth, and it didn't take long for the Bears and the rest of the NFL to realize it, either.

CLOSING THOUGHTS

WHEN I ENTERED into this project, my goal was simple—find out everything that takes place leading up to the NFL Draft to find out why things happen. I had my own experience leading me to be a bit puzzled about if there was a disconnect between coaches and general managers. While that exact scenario did not get a true answer due to the recent passing of Coach Dave Magazu, I was able to realize what I am sure you did as well while reading: A LOT CAN HAPPEN.

What I believe now is that Coach Magazu liked me as a prospect and wanted the opportunity to coach me. I always wondered if that Draft Day call in 2015 was just Coach blowing smoke, but due to the conversations with the coaches in this book I realized they can't always get what they want. Great organizations have to have a decision maker, which we learned is likely the general manager, and because of that a position coach only has so much power once the clock gets ticking.

I found that the NFL Draft has come a long way and you can see just how so with the many examples from this book. We see how Warren Moon had to be a trailblazer and pave the way for future African Americans at the quarterback position, helping to eliminate ludicrous stereotypes and narratives. We saw the complete overlooking of Steve Largent by not just what round he was selected in the NFL Draft, but the failure to see how to utilize him once getting him into your training camp. That exact scenario is sure to have been a case study and lesson for future scouts and teams to not let players like that out your door in such a brief time.

A major realization is how even first-round picks can enter Draft Day with not a clue in the world about where they will be selected. Even more surprising, a first-round pick can be selected by a team they barely had communication with during the pre-Draft process. As big of a deal as a first-round pick is, a player can still fall into a slot that even a team had not imagined they would, which ultimately can lead to a surprise pick.

When you watch the NFL Draft going forward do you feel like you have a better idea of the process? When the twenty-first pick in the Draft is at home with his family instead of on site at the Draft will you recall why an agent may recommend that? If your favorite team is in need of a wide receiver, yet they use their first-round pick on a linebacker, can you now piece together why that might be? If a player looks surprised by who drafted him, do you now understand that maybe he is just that?

If you don't have a better understanding of those scenarios among others then I have failed you. The eighteen legends involved in *ROUND ZERO: Inside the NFL Draft* have given us, through their own Draft stories, the deep dive into the pre-Draft process from every angle that allows us to have an ocean full of examples and scenarios to compare, contrast, and analyze future Drafts and picks.

We now know that there are four major angles that make the Draft what it is and shape what happens over those three days every spring. We have agents who we know aren't simply lawyers looking to make a quick buck. These are humans who care about seeing other humans succeed to their maximum potential both on and off the field. Agents are there to be masters of communication to help navigate their prospect through the most stressful part of their young careers, even if that means delivering bad news to ease the shock-factor on Draft Day. We also understand that general managers, at least the good ones, have a system in place that is the be-all-end-all so that structure outweighs emotion. We know the Board is the answer key on Draft Day and the best general managers let the

Board speak to them because they trust all of the work they did leading up to the Draft is on that Board and will lead them to make the best decisions for the football team. We see how coaches, who get involved later in the process than general managers and scouts, go about catching up and gathering as much information as they can. A tremendous amount of trust has to be had in the scouting department, but coaches also do their own evaluations and ultimately have a major say leading up to the Draft. When it comes to the players, I hope everyone came away with an appreciation for the amount of stress this has on young men. Imagine if the biggest job interview of your life was a four-month long process where you will be picked apart as much as possible on both a performance and personal level. Better yet, imagine if at the end of that interview process you had no clue what city you would end up in, if you even talked to your future bosses during the process, or even worse if you didn't get the job and would have to start job-hunting in a totally different industry. But yeah, football players' lives are all fun and games.

Now that you have the ultimate cheat sheet, are you ready for the next Draft? You better be because the clock is always ticking … until …

Time's up.

ACKNOWLEDGMENTS

A SPECIAL 'THANK YOU' to everyone who was interviewed for *Round Zero* and those that helped set up interviews, notably Rich Desrosiers, Michelle Norris, Tom Fanning, Jeff Durands, Julia Faron, Tyler Conklin, & Cooper Rush.

I would also like to thank my family and friends for always believing in my goals and aspirations.

Finally, I want to thank my wife, Alexis, for her ongoing support of my dreams and support along the way during this journey.

AUTHOR

Andy Phillips is a contributing writer at the Pro Football Hall of Fame. He is also a motivational speaker who speaks to a variety of audiences about the importance of character, perseverance, going after your goals, and the ability to view losses as lessons. He is a former 2x Division-1 Football Captain and played as an offensive lineman in four preseason NFL games with the Green Bay Packers.